TOURING IN WINE COUNTRY
BORDEAUX

MITCHELL BEAZLEY

TOURING IN WINE COUNTRY
BORDEAUX

HUBRECHT DUIJKER

SERIES EDITOR
HUGH JOHNSON

Contents

**Touring in Wine Country
Bordeaux**
published by Mitchell Beazley,
part of Reed Consumer Books Limited,
Michelin House, 81 Fulham Road,
London SW3 6RB
and Auckland, Melbourne, Singapore
and Toronto

First published in 1996
© Reed International Books Limited
1996
Text copyright © Hubrecht Duijker 1996
Maps copyright © Reed International
Books Limited 1996

Text adapted in part from 'Bordeaux – A
Wine Lover's Touring Guide' by Hubrecht
Duijker. First published 1993 by
Uitgeverij Het Spectrum BV

A CIP catalogue record of this book is
available from the British Library

ISBN 1 85732 558 3

Senior Editor: Susan Keevil
Editor: Lucy Bridgers
Art Editor: Paul Drayson
Senior Art Editor: Susan Downing
Index: Angie Hipkin
Gazetteer: Sally Chorley
Production: Juliette Butler
Managing Editor: Sue Jamieson
Art Director: Gaye Allen
Cartography: Map Creation Limited
Design by Bridgewater Book Company
Illustrations: Polly Raines

Typeset in Bembo and Gill Sans
Origination by Mandarin Offset,
Singapore
Produced by Mandarin Offset
Printed and bound in Hong Kong

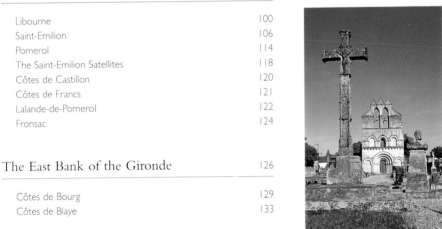

Foreword

Why is it that wine tasted in the cellar (or even in the region) of its birth has a magic, a vibrancy and vigour that makes it so memorable?

It is easy to think of physical reasons. The long journey to the supermarket shelf cannot be without some effect on a living creature – and wine is indeed alive, and correspondingly fragile.

It is even easier to think of romantic reasons: the power of association, the atmosphere and scents of the cellar, the enthusiasm of the grower as he moves from barrel to barrel...

No wonder wine touring is the first-choice holiday for so many people. It is incomparably the best way to understand wine whether at the simple level of its scenery and culture, or deeper into the subtleties of its *terroirs* and the different philosophies of different producers.

There are armchair wine-books, coffee-table books, quick reference wine-books... even a pop-up wine book. Now with this series we have the wine-traveller's precise, pin-pointed practical guide to sleuthing through the regions that have most to offer, finding favourites and building up memories. The bottles you find yourself have the genie of experience in them.

Hugh Johnson

A First
Acquaintance

The name Bordeaux has several applications: it is a city, a region, a wine, even a particular way of growing and making that wine. Bordeaux is, justifiably, the world's premier wine city. It has always led with regard to quality, as was already evident in 1855 with the first official classification of the Médoc and Sauternes *grands crus classés* châteaux. It was Bordeaux, too, that established a worldwide reputation for practically all aspects of scientific research into wine through its oenological institute. And not only this. *Barriques* – the 225-litre casks used worldwide for ageing wine – originated in Bordeaux. The region's traditional grape varieties are used throughout the world to improve the quality of local wines. And it is due to Bordeaux that the word *château* has become an honorary accolade. In short, Bordeaux is a phenomenon.

The city of Bordeaux is the sixth largest in France, and is the centre of the most renowned wine region in the world. Bordeaux lies on the Garonne River, which joins the Dordogne just north of the city, at Bourg. From this confluence the waterway is called the Gironde. It flows into the Atlantic between Le Verdon, at the most northerly point of the Médoc, and the town of Royan. The Médoc, Blaye and Bourg wine districts lie either side of the Gironde estuary.

The presence of these rivers is of the utmost importance for winegrowing, as the water serves to regulate air temperatures surrounding the vines. In the past they were also important as a means of transport – the development of the wine trade here is due in many ways to the rivers, and access to the open sea. The Atlantic Ocean makes itself felt in the rivers, for the ebb and flow of the tides is perceptible above Bordeaux and Libourne.

Left *The imposing entrance to Château Beychevelle in the commune of St-Julien. This fourth growth château has long been popular with the British and its wines in demand throughout the world.*

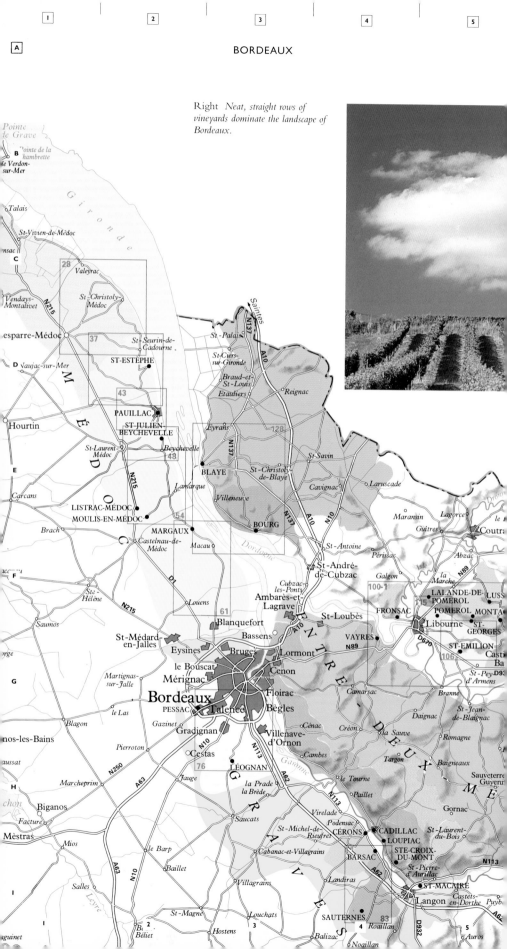

Right *Neat, straight rows of vineyards dominate the landscape of Bordeaux.*

CLIMATE

In Paris they are emphatic that Bordeaux has the best climate in France; this may well be true. Although the influence of the seasons is clearly observable, it is generally mild: the average winter temperature is 7.5°C while in summer it is 18°C. Hard frosts happen only occasionally but they can do considerable damage to the vines: in April 1991 night-time temperatures dropped to -11°C causing devastation in the vineyards – those close to the River Gironde were the least affected, thanks to its moderating influence.

There is certainly no lack of sun in Bordeaux; the average is 2,010 hours of sunshine per year, giving plenty of dry, warm weather for ripening the grapes – the not uncommon Indian summers are beneficial too. They say in Bordeaux '*Bel automne vient plus souvent que beau printemps*', and it is true that spring here can be fresh and damp, while autumn is often sunny. And such a climate is one of the most important factors behind Bordeaux's high quality.

SIGHTS TO SEE

Bordeaux's countryside is particularly appealing. Not only are the city and winegrowing districts well worth seeing, but so, too, is the coastal strip along the Atlantic. Dozens of miles of sandy beaches spread along the coast, behind which romantic lakes, conifer woods (Les Landes forest is the biggest in Europe), resorts and harbours await discovery. In summer here you can engage in practically any outdoor sport.

Lacanau is one of the coastal resorts – with a golf school and a fine course. Others well known are Soulac, Montalivet,

Bordeaux   F

– · – · – Département boundary	▨	Bourgeais
――――― Limit of Appellation Bordeaux	▨	Premieres Côtes de Bordeaux
☐ Haut-Médoc/St-Emilion	▨	Graves de Vayres
☐ Médoc/Pomerol	☐	Ste-Foy-Bordeaux/Côtes de Bordeaux-St-Macaire
☐ Canon-Fronsac/St-Emilion	☐	Graves
▨ Fronsac/Bordeaux et Entre-Deux-Mers-Haut-Benauge	☐	Cérons
▨ Côtes de Castillon	☐	Sauternes and Barsac
▨ Lalande-de-Pomerol/Côtes de Francs	☐	Loupiac
▨ Blayais	☐	Ste-Croix-du-Mont/Entre-Deux-Mers
☐ Pessac-Léognan		
	BOURG ●	Principal wine commune
	☐ 28	Area mapped at larger scale on page shown

1:570,000

Km. 0   5   10   15   20   25 Km.
Miles 0   5   10   15 Miles

Hourtain and Maubuisson, all tucked away among the never-ending coniferous woods. It would be wrong, by the way, to suppose that these woods are ancient. None of them was planted until the 19th century. Before this Les Landes was a boggy, almost inaccessible area where the inhabitants had to walk about on stilts in winter. Fortunately those days are long gone, and the conifers are now an important source of timber. All the railway lines laid down after the First World War to transport the logs for this have since been converted into cycleways, of which there are now several hundred kilometres to explore.

The Bassin d'Arcachon is another well-loved location. Home to an important nature reserve and many oyster farms, it looks like a lake, but actually has an outlet to the ocean. Famous places here are Arcachon itself – where many well-to-do Bordeaux wine-growers have apartments or second homes around the Bassin – the Gujan-Mestras, Cap Ferret, and Andernos.

Top *Working the vineyards at Château d'Yquem.*
Above *The harvest at châteaux Cos d'Estournel and* (right) *Lafite.*

Arcachon is a pleasant resort with its own distinctive aura. A strong period atmosphere prevails, so that at times you almost think yourself back in the 1920s. There is a pier from which boat trips out on the Bassin are run. To the south of Arcachon lies Pyla, with the highest sand-dune in Europe. Climbing it you might imagine yourself crossing the Sahara but, at the top, you look out over Arcachon and the Atlantic.

You can get to Arcachon from Bordeaux by the motorway that leads to Bayonne, or by the N250, leaving the ring road at Pessac. The former is quicker. You need to allow more time for the N250, but the advantage is it takes you to Gujan-Mestras and La Teste – where there is a large bird park and a butterfly garden. Although every little harbour around the Bassin has *cabanes* selling oysters, these are very much the speciality of Gujan-Mestras. There are also some excellent fish restaurants, and an important oyster festival.

The Bordeaux area is a paradise for lovers of golf. There are ten or so courses around the city where anyone may play. For walkers there are plenty of possible pathways in the pine forests and along the beaches. Those who like castles and abbeys will enjoy Entre-Deux-Mers; and for wine-lovers there are of course the viticultural districts and their many châteaux. All these attractions can be enjoyed within a radius of 50 to 80 kilometres of Bordeaux.

WINE ROUTES

The road most used for visiting the famous Médoc châteaux is the D2. This starts just outside Bordeaux (take the Le Verdon turning off the ring road, then turn right towards Pauillac). It winds through the Médoc to Saint-Vivien, passing many of the renowned *grands crus classés* châteaux (most of which

are described in this guide). Another recommended wine route goes from Bordeaux via the right bank of the Garonne through the Premières Côtes de Bordeaux: Bordeaux, Latresne, Camblanes, Quinsac, Cambes, Baurech, Tabanac, Le Tourne, Langoiran, Haux, Saint-Caprais, Cenac, and back to Bordeaux. This journey of some 55 kilometres takes you through one of the loveliest areas of the Bordelais. Signposting in the Sauternes, another district with its own wine route, is good and you can reach the area in less than half an hour from Bordeaux. This is a region famed for its idyllic and impressive estates. For routes around Saint-Emilion, the Graves and Entre-Deux-Mers refer to the relevant chapters.

WINEGROWING AND WINES

The Bordeaux wine region covers about 115,000 hectares. This makes it five times as big as Burgundy and as extensive as all the vineyards of Germany or South Africa. Yet in the mid-19th century the total area was even greater. The decrease was due to devastation wrought by the phylloxera insect and the spread of towns and villages. Wine is of such great importance to Bordeaux, however, that almost 110,000 hectares of *appellation contrôlée* vineyards exist there.

All in all there are some 13,000 winegrowers: 5,000 belong to cooperatives, and there are 400 wine firms. Put into a more personal perspective, one in six people in the Gironde works with wine. Château vineyards average at about five hectares – many are half this size, and very few exceed 20 – and 75 percent of them are for red wine, 25 percent white. There are 53 *appellations contrôlées*, which cover red, dry white, sweet white, rosé, *clairet* (light red) and *crémant* (sparkling) wines.

THE CLASSIFICATIONS

The 1800s in the Médoc saw most châteaux come into being and also the first official wine classification in 1855. Expertise was pooled to elevate 88 châteaux to *grand cru classé* status. Médoc *crus* were subdivided into three *premiers crus*, 15 *deuxièmes crus* (second growths), 14 *troisièmes*, ten *quatrièmes* and 18 *cinquièmes*. These categories are still used, along with 'cru bourgeois' for the next level down. For Sauternes there was one *premier cru supérieur* (Château d'Yquem), 11 *premiers crus* and 15 *deuxièmes crus*. After World War II two further

classifications were created: that of Graves, with 15 *crus classés*, and Saint-Emilion's, now with 63 *grands crus classés* and 11 *premiers grands crus classés* (two 'A's and nine 'B's).

GRAPE VARIETIES

Unlike the wines of other wine regions, such as Alsace and Burgundy, Bordeaux wines are always made from more than one grape variety. The properties of these grapes complement each other, and after vinification and the final blending a wine is obtained that is highly characteristic of its appellation. One Bordeaux wine will always be different from another.

The varieties used have remained practically unchanged since the Middle Ages. For red wine the grapes are: Merlot, Cabernet Sauvignon, Cabernet Franc, Malbec and Petit Verdot. For white: Sauvignon Blanc, Sémillon, Muscadelle, Colombard and Ugni Blanc. Differences between these varieties are substantial. The Cabernet Sauvignon, for instance, is harvested later than Merlot, so has longer to ripen and can often benefit from warm weather in October. Broadly, Merlot could be said to give suppleness to its wine, where Cabernet Sauvignon lends more body ('*corps*'), and tannin. (A useful insight into Bordeaux style comes from the fact that Cabernet predominates in the Médoc, while Saint-Emilion and Pomerol are largely Merlot's domain.) Malbec and Petit Verdot had to some extent disappeared from the scene but, thanks to current oenological thinking, they seem to be making something of a comeback. However, they usually represent no more than two to three percent of the grapes grown – although there may be more Malbec in Côtes de Bourg and Blaye, even as much as 30 percent.

The difference between the white varieties Sauvignon and Sémillon is greater than that between Cabernet and Merlot. Sauvignon gives fresh, fragrant lively wines; Sémillon wines are more rounded, supple and powerful. Sweet wines are made from both. Other whites are somewhat simpler in style.

SOIL

A mild climate and high-quality grapes would be of little significance without good soil. Soils of various compositions occur in the Gironde. This of course is one of the reasons for the differences between the wines. Many layers of soil were brought down by the rivers in primeval times, notably gravels from the Pyrenees, the Massif Central and other upland areas. Various kinds of gravel became mixed together, and in certain places deep accumulations occurred. These '*croupes*', offer an excellent and varied medium for vine roots – and perfect drainage. The Médoc has many of these gravel hills, and they occur in the Graves and Saint-Emilion, too.

In other parts of Bordeaux the vines are hardly less well off: on soils of limestone, clay, sand, or mixtures of these. The limestone slopes of Saint-Emilion and clay plateau of Pomerol show that great wines can come from other soils, too.

Top Cabernet Sauvignon grapes give the wine body and tannin, not to mention the typical blackcurrant and cedarwood flavours.
Left Merlot grapes are thinner skinned than Cabernet and best suited to heavier, clay soils.
Above Sémillon grapes which have been attacked by the highly desirable 'Noble Rot'; this dehydrates the grape, concentrating the grape sugars.

THE HUMAN FACTOR

Finally there is the human factor, without which good wine could never be produced. The unremitting toil of the wine-grower is of the utmost importance for achieving good quality. The grower is busy the whole year through with wine and vine, in the vineyard or in the *chais*. He, or she, determines the ultimate quality by deciding (among other things) on the moment for picking, the choice of grapes, the method of wine fermentation, and the treatment of the wine.

THE CUISINE

Wine and gastronomy go together: wine is made to accompany the courses and enhance the content of a meal. In Bordeaux there is an added dimension in the presence of the châteaux – for many wine-lovers, being invited to a meal at a château is an honour and a festive occasion.

The owners, it is true, do not always live in their châteaux, but they like receiving guests there. Not so long ago you could make an appointment for a tasting and be automatically invited for lunch; but, alas, those days are gone. The keynote of such a meal is usually the traditional regional cuisine: thus duck's liver (*foie gras de canard*), grilled entrecôtes of lamb, cheese and dessert are likely to be frequently served.

Main picture and above right
Bordeaux is renowned for its
wonderful fresh seafood which goes so
well with Entre-Deux-Mers wines.

Food shopping in and around
Bordeaux is excellent for anything
from bread (above left) to specialities
such as charcuterie (below).

The food always tastes good, and there is also the privilege of being able to drink the wines of several vintages from the château in question. A meal like this remains a unique event, and is guaranteed to show off the wine at its very best.

As to dishes, the regional cuisine of Bordeaux has much to offer. There is lamb from Pauillac; oysters from the Bassin d'Arcachon (often eaten here with a *crépinette*, a small sausage); duck and the specialities derived from it, from neighbouring Gers; asparagus from Blaye; beef (*blonde d'Aquitaine*) from Bazas; sea fish, crustaceans and shellfish from the Atlantic; sausages (*boudins*) from Lormont; lamprey and white shrimps from the Gironde; the sweet *canalés* from Bordeaux; and Saint-Emilion macaroons. It could be said that all that is lacking is a local cheese. The Bordelais reply that they are happy to avail themselves of farm cheese from Holland, 'the other cheese country'.

Worthy of separate mention is the entrecôte *grillée aux sarments de vigne* – sirloin (or rib of beef, or lamb cutlets) grilled over smouldering vine twigs. Even the very greatest red wines show to full advantage with this country dish. It is also one of the traditional meals served to grape-pickers during the harvest – quite often as a breakfast. Very special, too, is lamprey in a red-wine sauce, *lamproie à la Bordelaise*. This curious, elongated predatory fish still frequents the Gironde, where it may be caught in limited numbers in the spring. Lampreys are usually potted and may be bought in Kilner-type jars from delicatessens or *traiteurs* – they are said to gain flavour with time in bottle. There used to be sturgeon in the river, too, and caviare was produced from it in the little town of Blaye. Today, however, fishing for sturgeon is strictly prohibited, and efforts to encourage the fish back are being made. *Chevrettes* are another speciality. These white, almost transparent shrimps are eaten with aperitifs and can be bought in the *guinguettes* (country taverns) along the rivers.

How to Use this Guide

In words and pictures this guide takes you through practically all the wine districts of Bordeaux. As we have seen, this is regarded as the biggest quality wine-producing region in the world. A fact which makes the details here all the more valuable. For each wine town or village the most important things to see are carefully reported. Thus in Saint-Emilion, for example, the book will guide you round the most notable of its monuments, and pick out other items of interest, such as shops where you can buy regional delicacies.

Outside the larger communities, Bordeaux has only a modest number of good hotels. This is why for some places an address for *chambres d'hôte* (accommodation in private rooms) is given. Restaurants are listed, including some very simple and affordable ones. Some of the places to stay and places to eat are not to be found in any other guide – which of course does not mean that spending time in them would be anything other than pleasant. The hotel prices given refer in principle to double rooms without breakfast. Restaurant prices represent the cheapest set menus, without drinks.

The best winemakers for each district are listed, too. This is a very modest selection of all the châteaux and cooperatives in Bordeaux, but it amounts to hundreds nevertheless.

Above A vineyard in Fronsac. This pretty commune is just west of St-Emilion and produces wines from the same grape varieties: Merlot and Cabernet Franc.

MAPS

Right *Detailed wine maps showing commune boundaries, Crus Classés, and other vineyard boundaries are included, complete with suggested wine routes. These routes take in the most important villages and vineyards, but if you have time, do try to explore further.*

HOTEL RESERVATIONS

When making a hotel reservation always ask for a quiet room at the back, or facing the courtyard if there is one. Look out for any nearby church bells likely to ring loudly and often. When reserving a room you will usually be given a latest time to book in. Should you be thinking of arriving later, ring up on the day to let the hotel know – otherwise there is a chance you will lose your room. Written confirmation of your reservation may be prudent. Do this by letter, or by fax – ask for the number. Lists of private persons who rent out rooms (*gîtes* or *chambres d'hôte*) are usually kept at the town hall or its equivalent, or the *office du tourisme*.

RESTAURANTS – EATING OUT IN BORDEAUX

Telephoning a restaurant in advance is always to be recommended: both to be sure of a table and to check that it is open that day. Experience tells that it generally makes sense to order set menus, not only for their relatively low prices, but also because their ingredients will often be fresh from market. In the simpler eating houses it is best mainly to choose regional dishes, as complicated recipes from elsewhere may overtax the chef. And always aim to choose the regional wines, if possible from the district you are in. These will have been selected more expertly and critically than wines from other appellations – let alone those from areas outside Bordeaux. A carafe of water is always free, and mineral waters can be ordered.

MEETING THE GROWERS AND VISITING THE CHATEAUX

It may take a good deal of effort to get to see the famous growers, particularly if they have no problems in selling their wines at high prices. There are, too, quite a few wine-producing châteaux where it is made clear that visitors are not wanted. However, do not give up too quickly, for if you are truly interested in wine, and make this apparent, most doors will be open to you. (Showing this guide may help: anyone who arrives thus recommended will usually have a friendlier reception than someone who casually drops in.)

When tasting wines it is quite customary to spit them out – but ask first where you can do this. Ask, too, what you should do with any drops left in the glass; sometimes the producer has a special container for these.

And never tip winegrowers; but buy at least one bottle from them as a token of appreciation for the hospitality enjoyed. French will generally be the only medium of communication, although nowadays many young winegrowers do speak English.

THE CITY OF BORDEAUX

WINE SHOPS

Badie
62 Allées de Tourny; Tel: 56 52 23 72
Bordeaux Magnum
3 Rue Gobineau; Tel: 56 48 00 06
Le Dépôt des Châteaux
37 Rue Esprit des Lois; Tel: 56 44 03 92
L'Intendant
2 Allées de Tourny; Tel: 56 48 01 29
Savour Club
72 Quai Bacalan; Tel: 56 39 87 67
La Vinothèque
8 Cours du 30 Juillet; Tel: 56 77 10 88

HOTELS

Burdigala
116 Rue Georges Bonnat
Tel: 56 90 16 16
Ideally situated in the centre, with
spacious, nicely decorated rooms. Prices
around FF800; suites from FF1200.
Château Chartrons
81 Cours Saint-Louis; Tel: 56 43 15 00
Fine hotel, but you need transport into
the centre. Prices from FF700.
Claret
Cité Mondiale; Tel: 56 01 79 79
By the quayside and in the old district
of Chartrons. Prices around FF500.

Main picture *The Fontaine
des Trois Graces in the Place de
la Bourse.*
Above right *The dramatic spire
of the Eglise St-Michel.*
Above *One of the numerous cafés
in the centre of Bordeaux, ideal for
either sampling some of the region's
wide variety of wines or simply
watching the world go by.*

The City of Bordeaux

B ordeaux is the most important eco-
nomic centre in southwest France.
Despite all the activity this entails, at
a European level it is no longer so
significant in its traditional role as a
port. The Bordeaux quaysides are still
a powerful tourist attraction, and
quite often cruise ships tie up oppo-
site the beautiful Place de la Bourse. As a result of the
reduced shipping trade, however, many dockside sheds now
stand empty. If these often dilapidated buildings were to be
pulled down, the Quai des Chartrons might regain its former
lustre, for it is here that most of the wine merchants were
originally established. A good deal of restoration work has
already been done, and many frontages cleaned. The opening
of Bordeaux's southern ring road has, happily, put a stop to
much of the heavy freight traffic.

Wine is especially important for the Bordeaux economy,
but there are also other sources of income, from agriculture
and industry (aviation, ship building, oil, chemicals, metals
and space technology). The city is becoming increasingly pop-

ular as a conference and exhibition centre, too. Just outside Bordeaux some vast exhibition halls have been built. Vinexpo, the world's biggest wine fair, is held in these halls every other year.

THE ARCHITECTURE

Many people visiting Bordeaux for the first time compare it to Paris. Indeed part of the city is characterized by 18th-century buildings, broad avenues and boulevards (here called *allées*) in a similar style. Alternatively, French author Victor Hugo wrote 'Take Versailles, add to it Antwerp and you have Bordeaux'. Such comparisons hold far less weight today. Bordeaux has been afflicted by urban development – making it possible, for instance, for a contemporary shopping and office complex called the Mériadeck to be built right next to La Chartreuse, one of France's most splendid 19th-century town cemeteries. Evenings are now dark and forebodingly quiet in both.

Nevertheless, Bordeaux does have much that is beautiful to offer: the aforementioned Place de la Bourse, the Allées de Tourny (once a vineyard), where the striking Maison du Vin stands, and the Grand Théâtre nearby (built by Victor Louis, architect of the Paris Opéra). And no description of Bordeaux can leave out the Place (or Esplanade) des

Mercure Bordeaux Lac
Avenue J-G Domergue; *Tel: 56 50 90 30*
Outside city, by the exhibition area. A practical choice. Prices from FF330.

Normandie
7 Cours du 30 Juillet; *Tel: 56 52 60 44*
Classic hotel beside the Maison du Vin. Prices from about FF320.

Royal Médoc
5 Rue Sère; *Tel: 56 81 72 42*
Hotel with atmosphere and an agreeable bar. Prices around FF280.

RESTAURANTS

Baud et Millet
19 Rue Hugurie; *Tel: 56 79 05 77*
Restaurant and a shop for wine and cheese. Many non-French wines and a lot of cheese. Set menus from FF85.

Quinconces: a remarkable raised urban 'plateau'. Here various events are organized, from fairs and *Quatorze Juillet* celebrations, to antique and flower markets. Also impressive is the great fountain monument to the Girondists. And then the Place du Parlement, with almost a village character.

The old heart of the city, *le vieux Bordeaux*, is quietly being restored; you will find more and more art galleries setting up, and unexpected, curious little shops and places to eat. And if a structure is demolished, then the city's antiquities service is there ready to carry out archaeological investigations before there can be any new building. Because of this, more and more details of Roman life are coming to light, and these are rarely better illustrated than by the Palais Gallien with the remains of a 3rd-century Roman amphitheatre.

At the opposite extreme, the Cité Mondiale du Vin et des Spiritueux on the Quai des Chartrons (not far from the Place des Quinconces) is totally new. It is an imposing office block of stainless steel and glass, intended as a trade centre for wines and spirits. There are showrooms with wines from various parts of the world and monthly exhibitions on different

Top *A traditional street sign for one of Bordeaux's many food shops.*
Above *The bustling Rue Ste-Catherine in the centre of the city.*
Right *Sunset over le Pont de Pierre Lampadaires.*

Le Bistro du Sommelier
167 Rue Georges Bonnac
Tel: 56 96 71 78
The owner is a well-known cellarman. His wine knowledge is reflected in the always fascinating list: good *grands crus classés* for less than FF150 a bottle, many great names sold by the glass. A simple, tasty three-course set menu costs around FF100.

La Chamade
20 Rue des Piliers-de-Tutelle
Tel: 56 48 13 74
Here below the 18th-century arches is one of Bordeaux's best restaurants. Set menus from FF180, and wines from St-Julien and St-Emilion.

Le Chapon Fin
5 Rue Montesquieux
Tel: 56 79 10 10
One of the best restaurants in south-west France; owner Francis Garcia is a great culinary figure in Bordeaux. His restaurant is luxuriously furnished. Set lunch menus around FF135, with others up to about FF400. Excellent wine list with many affordable items.

wine themes. In its hall there is a remarkable wall made up of bottles, reflecting all the colours of wine.

SHOPS AND MARKETS

Shopping in Bordeaux calls for some discernment. The Rue Sainte-Cathérine is one of the best spots: a long street – about 1,100 metres long, packed with department stores and specialist shops. There is ample parking space nearby, near the Place des Quinconces and below the Allées de Tourny.

Modern shopping centres are the Mériadeck, in the city and with a covered car park, and the Bordeaux-Lac or Mérignac, by the airport. In the centre of Bordeaux there is the relatively new (and expensive) Les Grands Hommes: a handsome building with shops on three storeys, and a car park below. The name is derived from the original Grands Hommes daily market held in the Allées de Tourny.

Anyone who loves markets should visit the Marché des Capuchins. From 5am you can buy fresh produce here in the company of Bordeaux's great chefs. This lies in the oldest quarter, near the Place de la Victoire, 'the belly of Bordeaux'.

For the best chocolate, the Bordelais go to Saunion shop, at 56 Cours Georges-Clémenceau, where three generations of craftsmanship provide marvellous confectionery. And for the best cheese, go to Jean d'Alose in Rue Montesquieu. The shop at 25 Rue Camille-Sauvageau is tasteful, pleasant and Flemish, and belongs to Jan Demaitre, a true baker.

Top *Elegant architecture dominates Bordeaux's centre.*
Above *Fresh local produce on sale at one of the city's markets.*

Le Dégustoir
8 Rue André Dumercq
Belongs to an idealistic oenologist and thus perfect for wine-lovers. Many unfamiliar wines by the glass. Simple menu. Recommended is the *plateau fond de barrique*. Friendly, relaxed.
Didier Gélineau
26 Rue de Pas-Saint-Georges
Tel: 56 52 84 25
A place to spend time; attractive prices. Set menus around FF100.
Pavillon des Boulevards
120 Rue de la Croix-de-Seguey
Tel: 56 81 51 02
More expensive but good. Modern-classic cuisine. Menus about FF300.

Chez Philippe
I Place Parlement
Tel: 56 81 83 15
One of the very best places to go
for fish, shellfish, crab and lobster. An
interesting set menu at about FF185,
but offering a choice of four starters,
four main courses and four desserts.

Le Rouzie
34 Cours du Chapeau-Rouge
Tel: 56 44 39 11
The Gautiers, a married couple, have a
good division of labour: he is a wizard
in the kitchen, she is responsible for
the wine list; both have talent.
Remarkably unfamiliar regional wines,
supplied at a low profit margin. Set
menus start around FF140.

La Tupina
6 Rue Porte de la Monnaie
Tel: 56 91 56 37
One of the most original cuisines in
Bordeaux, under the management of
the dynamic and inventive Jean-Pierre
Xiradakis; with certain dishes he even
supplies the name of the butcher. A
sumptuous, nostalgic atmosphere,
regional specialities and a very good
list with affordable wines. Set menus
from about FF140. Very good service.

BUYING WINE

For anyone going to the Bordeaux region who
wants to buy wine, even if only to be able to
say it was actually purchased there, a number
of ways are possible: directly from a château, at
specialist shops, or from a hypermarket. Most
of the *grands crus classés* châteaux do not sell 'on
the premises', but many *crus bourgeois* do –
though prices are certainly no more favourable
this way. Buying in a shop has the advantage
that you can make comparisons. For a long
time the most obvious shop to do this was La Vinothèque,
right opposite the Maison du Vin. Others are Badie,
Bordeaux Magnum, and L'Intendant. Badie is an old-estab-
lished name in Bordeaux. Bordeaux Magnum, at the back of
the Maison du Vin, is a bright, fully air-conditioned place
with a large selection, the emphasis being on wines from the
Pessac and Léognan districts of Graves; it even has a Tokyo
branch. L'Intendant is a spectacular affair where you go
down spiral stairs, the vintages getting older as you descend.
Then, in the Cité Mondiale, there is a branch of Nicolas.
Another interesting shop is the sales section of the Savour
Club on the Quai Bacalan. Savour Club is a wine mail order
firm, with tasting and retail facilities in a number of towns.
You can become a member free of charge even if you intend
only to make one purchase a year. And Le Dépôt des
Châteaux is a fairly new little shop in old Bordeaux, with
many lesser-known wines at château prices.

Finally, a probably unexpected tip: buy your wine at a
supermarket. Knowing that 60 percent of the French public
do just this could well be an extra inducement. Leclerc-
Candéran and Leclerc-Léognan have a good to excellent
choice of wine, the latter, apparently, with the largest wine
department in France.

Far left (top) *Part of the Monument des Girondins, celebrating Bordeaux's commercial importance of the early 19th-century.* Far left (bottom) *Bordeaux is a haven for lovers of fish and seafood.* Left *Another of Bordeaux's markets, here, in front of the medieval town gate.*

Le Vieux Bordeaux
27 Rue Buhan
Tel: 56 52 94 36
In the heart of old Bordeaux is this atmospheric restaurant with brass candlesticks and red plush chairs. For years now there has been an excellent price-to-quality relationship. Set menus from around FF170. A substantial wine list with many great names.

RESTAURANTS: BORDEAUX AREA

ARCACHON
Chez Yvette
59 boulevard Général Leclerc
Tel: 56 83 05 11
The best-known restaurant here with all the good things from the Bassin and the sea. Madame Yvette's fish soup is a speciality. Set menus around FF85.

ARES
St-Eloi
Near the water and the best place to eat on the north side of the Bassin, between Biganos and Cap Ferret. Classic regional, honest-to-goodness cooking. Set menus from about FF110. Good, reasonably priced wine list.

GUJAN-MESTRAS
La Guérinière
Splendid hotel-restaurant with a friendly bar and a swimming pool. Good classic cuisine. Set menus from around FF125. Modern, comfortable rooms with terrace from FF365.
Les Viviers
Tel: 56 66 01 04
The Castaings have been a family of oyster farmers and restaurateurs for five generations. Their fish restaurant is uniquely situated on the harbour. First floor is recommended. Set menu from about FF120 from 12 noon, and specialities of the day are written up on a board. Oysters here are marvellous; the fish dishes delicious and classic: *Plateau de fruits de mer* (around FF120) is the speciality. The simple, straightforward wine list is well attuned to the fish dishes served.

HOTELS

Ten years ago hotel accommodation was rather scarce and disappointing for a city of this size. The picture has changed totally. Familiar hotel chains are now all present, and for tourists passing through, the Formule 1 hotels are popular as you only pay about FF150 for a room for three. In the centre of the city, too, there is now ample choice. The hotels Normandie and Royal Médoc are pleasant, somewhat old-fashioned, and well situated. But Bordeaux's best is probably the Burdigala, very comfortable and very expensive. Alternatively, for those keen to immerse themselves fully in the world of wine, the luxurious Château Chartrons or the Claret Hotel in the Cité Mondiale are good choices.

RESTAURANTS

Eating out in this city is a great pleasure, for there are places to dine in all price categories. From 12.30pm it is often difficult to get a free table in any well-known establishment, but one of the attractions of lunch is that set menus may be lower in price than in the evenings. When there are so many restaurants, any recommendation is by definition a mere snapshot of limited validity, but there is an abundance of good, honest, often delightful food and drink to discover.

The Médoc

The Médoc is a tapering, triangular peninsula northwest of Bordeaux, bordered by the Atlantic Ocean and the Gironde, whose influences combine to create a microclimate often ideal for vines. The name Médoc is derived from the Latin *in medio aquae*, 'in the midst of the waters'.

In the geographical centre of the peninsula at Saint-Seurin-de-Cadourne lies the border between the Haut-Médoc and Médoc – also the division between the two wine appellations bearing these names. The latter used to be called Bas-Médoc, but as this had a somewhat negative ring the 'Bas' has been dropped. If you look at the map you will see that Haut-Médoc lies in the south, nearer to Bordeaux. The two districts have equal areas of vineyard – about 3,500 hectares each – but in the world of wine Haut-Médoc is rated rather higher.

Winegrowing in the Médoc did not begin until the 16th century, after prosperous merchants established wine estates of some importance there: the earliest ones were in Macau and Margaux. From the 18th century it was increasingly ear-marked as a wine district, signs of wealth appearing in the form of village churches and country houses. By the early 19th century most of the châteaux were beginning to be built.

Today the area's economy depends on two important ele-ments: winegrowing and tourism (the latter centred mainly on the Atlantic coast). The number of wine enthusiasts coming to the Médoc is growing considerably, with the result that more and more attention is being paid to facili-ties for recreation and château visits. In the summer many châteaux now open their *chais* and often put on exhibitions.

A visitor seeking evening entertainment should, though, look for it in Bordeaux not in the Médoc, for the peninsula is silent and deserted after sunset.

Left Château Beychevelle in of St-Julien. This commune has the highest concentration of classed growths in the Médoc and its wines strike a balance between the structure and brilliance of Pauillac, to the north, and the refined, perfumed ele-gance of Margaux, further south.

Northern Médoc

The northern part of the Médoc, with the village of Saint-Seurin-de-Cadourne at its southern boundary, is profiled here. It used to be called Bas-Médoc as it lies on the lower, downstream reaches of the River Gironde: *bas*, meaning 'low'. This sounds less than flattering when it comes to wine, and so plain Médoc is used instead.

Many visitors to the *grands crus classés* travel no further north than Saint-Estèphe, or even turn back at Château Cos d'Estournel. They are of course wrong to do this, for the Médoc is a land full of surprises and discoveries. Not only can you find lovely, relatively affordable wines, but this is also an attractive countryside to visit. Roaming this northern part of the peninsula, set between ocean and river, it is almost possible to believe you are in the Camargue, or the south of France, or even on a Dutch polder.

This is a land of distant views and of water, of meadows and of canals – especially canals. And these do indeed have a Dutch, or rather a Dutch and Flemish, history to them. Until the 17th century the Médoc was a doomed and ghostly land full of woe, '*une terre de misère*'. The low-lying parts were often under water, and malaria wrought great havoc. The disease was even called Médoquine. In fact the Médoc consisted then of various large, seemingly inaccessible islands. In 1628 the Duke of Epernon commissioned Flemish and Dutch water engineers to link them by banking up stretches of the flooded land. The polders then came into being and the canals were dug to drain reclaimed areas. (The word 'polder'

Northern Médoc

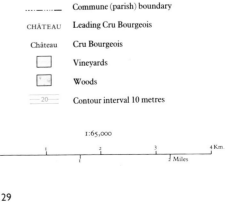

Wine route	
Canton boundary	
Commune (parish) boundary	
CHÂTEAU	Leading Cru Bourgeois
Château	Cru Bourgeois
	Vineyards
	Woods
—20—	Contour interval 10 metres

1:65,000

Km. 0   1   2   3   4 Km.
Miles 0   1   Miles

NORTHERN MEDOC

HOTELS

GAILLAN-EN-MEDOC
Château Layauga
Luxury hotel-restaurant, with seven
rooms at prices from around FF520.
Amazingly good cuisine with classic
dishes of great refinement. A great
relief to find this here in the Médoc.
Set menus start at around FF200.
In autumn the cèpes au jus de truffes
are delightful. There is an excellent
wine list.

QUEYRAC
Hôtel des Vieux Acacias
Tel: 56 59 80 63
Nice hotel in its own little park, for
which it has won awards. A breakfast
surprise here is the melon jam. Room
prices from about FF220.

RESTAURANT

ST-CHRISTOLY
La Maison du Douanier
Tel: 56 41 35 25
Near the harbour, the terrace has
views over the river. Regional
specialities at affordable prices. Open
every day in in July and August.

Main picture *Pastoral life on a
farm in St-Seurin in the Médoc.*
Above *Ducks and geese are farmed
for foie gras, which combines perfectly
with Sauternes.*
Far right *Château la Tour de By,
a cru bourgeois with an increasing
following for its quality and value.*

has remained in the French vocabulary
since that time.) The drained marshes
around Queyrac and Goulée acquired
the name Polder de Hollande, and
sometimes they were referred to as La
Petite Flandre du Médoc. An 18th-
century windmill near the village of
Vensac – still in use as a watermill – can
be visited on Sunday afternoons from
March to the end of September.

Not all the area is low-lying: there are
higher parts made up of gravel and sand.
These were eventually recognised as
especially suitable for winegrowing. Excellent vineyards are
often to be found on these gently sloping *croupes*.

Along the Atlantic shore are the dunes, vast masses of
sand which, with their great stretches of beach, draw many
tourists. This west coast of the Médoc is totally different
from the reclaimed land along the river. Here the scene is
one of mighty ocean breakers, great inland lakes (such as Lac

Le Relais chez Monique

Tel: 56 69 25 15

Simple *routiers* restaurant on the N215. Set lunchtime menu at around FF65, including wine.

Valeyrac/Port de Goulée La Guinguette

Tel: 56 41 37 48

A tremendously old-fashioned eating house by the harbour. A dozen oysters cost less than FF50.

RECOMMENDED PRODUCERS

BEGADAN

Château de By

Cru Bourgeois (By)

Tel: 56 41 51 53

Deep-coloured wine of good quality, needing some time to develop.

Château La Clare

Cru Bourgeois (Condissas)

Tel: 56 41 50 61

Intensely coloured, well-made Médoc with delicious red berry fruit on the finish.

Château La Croix Landon

A good average Médoc, supple and pleasant tasting.

Château Greysac

Cru Bourgeois

Tel: 56 73 26 56

Château for smooth, harmonious, easy-to-drink wines.

Château Laujac

Cru Bourgeois

Tel: 56 41 50 12

A dark, reserved wine, rich in tannin and needing some time to mature.

d'Hourtin), conifer forests and holiday resorts. Up at the most northerly point of the Médoc you can look across to the 'mainland' and the harbour and resort of Royan. And in Le Verdon, a little village with a harbour near the Pointe de Grave, stands the Cordouan lighthouse, France's oldest. It even contains a royal chamber and a small chapel. Pointe de Grave is quite a popular spot for ornithologists as it is a good site to watch the northerly migration of birds in spring.

There are no vineyards near this northern tip. The Médoc's most northern vineyards are to be found a little way south in Jau, Dignac, Vensac, and Loirac. These are wine enclaves in the polders – a fact in itself to make them worth seeing. Between Dignac and Goulée you can turn onto the D102E, which runs in a straight line through the Polder de Hollande to Queyrac.

Château Patache d'Aux
Cru Bourgeois
Tel: 56 41 50 18
The château is situated in the centre of Bégadan on the spot where stagecoaches used to stop. The wine continues to improve but is already a pleasant, full-bodied mouthful when young.

Château Plagnac
Tel: 56 31 44 44
Elegant Médoc with a good colour and long length.

THE VINEYARDS

The grape varieties used in the Médoc AC are the same as in other districts of the peninsula. Permissable yields are a little higher than in Haut-Médoc, but many of the growers strive for better quality and often observe the most stringent possible standards. For those who are not averse to adventure in wine, and value personal contact with growers, the Médoc appellation is a good place to go. They will generally be cordially received and wine prices are mostly reasonable.

As in the Haut-Médoc there are quite a few *crus bourgeois*, but there is also a large number of *crus artisans*. Although

Right and far right Oysters are a local delicacy. A large percentage is farmed in the peaceful Bassin d'Arcachon, an inlet of the Atlantic Ocean, southwest of the city of Bordeaux.
Below The impressive entrance to Château Tour de By. A well-structured wine is produced here, but one which is nevertheless remarkably approachable in its youth.

Château Rollan de By
Tel: 56 41 58 59
Visits by appointment.
Château St-Saturnin
Supple, rounded wine with not too much tannin.
Château La Tour de By
Cru Bougeois
Tel: 56 41 50 03
There are two châteaux here. The smaller, Château La Roque de By, dates from the 18th century, the larger from the 19th. Close to the vineyard stands a former light tower – worth climbing for the panoramic view. Remarkably good wine with a deep red colour and a stylish palate.
Cooperative
Tel: 56 41 50 13
The Médoc wine, Cave St-Jean, is firm and fairly tannic.
Vieux Château Landon
Cru Bourgeois
Tel: 56 41 50 42
Well-structured, supple wine, enjoyable after just two to three years.

back in the 19th century the *cru paysan* and *cru artisan* were described in the standard work *Bordeaux et ses vins* (Cocks & Ferret 1850 edition), the use of these terms on labels has always been forbidden. This is now to change. A syndicate of *cru artisan* growers has been set up, duly acknowledged by the French agricultural ministry. It seems likely that the European Community will sanction the term, too. In French the word *artisan* means 'craftsman' and thus describes products made in a non-industrial way. A craftsman-like wine will come from a small estate – and this is generally the case with *crus artisans* – with three to four hectares of vineyard. This, along with certain quality requirements, is taken into account when the wines are considered for *cru artisan* status. Many owners of a *cru artisan* run their vineyards just as sidelines or hobbies.

THE WINE ROUTES

There are various routes for exploring the Médoc. A good way is to begin on the D2 at Saint-Vivien-de-Médoc in the north. The advantage of this road is that it will take you to the little harbours of Goulée, By and Saint-Christoly. The restaurant on the harbour at Goulée is a must. Other sites worth seeing are the old lighthouse on the estate of Château La Tour de By, and Bégadan with its historic church with an 11th-century apse. At Château Loudenne, where you can have lunch if you arrange it beforehand, there is a collection of winegrowing equipment and tools. This estate also makes a white wine. Lesparre, the 'capital' of this part of the Médoc, is a small market town with a congenial atmosphere. The square, 14th-century tower here, l'Honneur de Lesparre, is a historic monument. Information about the area and its wines can be obtained from the Maison du Médoc.

Then head across to Saint-Seurin-de-Cadourne to begin exploring the Haut-Médoc.

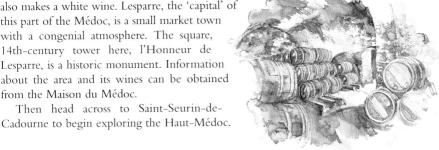

Top *An elegant stairway leads up to Château la Lagune in Ludon.* Main picture *Fishing nets are a common sight on the Gironde.* Right *Château Bel-Air Lagrave, Moulis. This* cru bourgeois *produces charming wines with good fruitiness.*

ST-SEURIN-DE-CADOURNE

 HOTEL

Tel: 56 59 54 03
In Cissac Château Vieux-Branaire has guest rooms from around FF200.

 RECOMMENDED PRODUCERS

Châteaux Coufran and Verdignan
Cru Bourgeois
Tel: 56 59 31 02 or 56 44 90 84
An unusually high proportion of Merlot is used for Château Coufran. Verdignan is stylish and elegant.
Château Sociando-Mallet
Cru Bourgeois
Tel: 56 59 36 57
This stylish blend of Cabernet and Merlot is a top *crus bourgeois* wine.

VERTHEUIL

 RECOMMENDED PRODUCERS

Château le Bourdieu
Cru Bourgeois
Tel: 56 41 98 01
A visit can include a look at the 17th-century abbey of Vertheuil.
Château Le Meynieu
Cru Bourgeois
Tel: 56 41 98 17
Group visits by appointment.

Northern Haut-Médoc

Haut-Médoc is one of the two regional appellations of the peninsula (the other being Médoc, as we have seen). The Haut-Médoc begins at the northern boundary of the village of Saint-Seurin-de-Cadourne, and ends a few kilometres north of Bordeaux, near Château Magnol – the entire appellation covering about 3,500 vineyard hectares. Although its territory forms an entity, interrupted just here and there by smaller appellations, in this guide the north and south of the Haut-Médoc appellation are described separately, with the division made at Saint-Laurent.

Starting in the north of the territory (at Saint-Seurin-de-Cadourne) you can travel south back towards Bordeaux past some of the most fascinating wine sights of the entire region. First, you'll need to decide where to begin: either explore the 'Bas-Médoc' first (see pages 29–33), or head to Saint-Seurin and embark on the wine route from there.

To the west of Saint-Seurin-de-Cadourne, the three villages of Vertheuil, Cissac, and Saint-Sauveur form the border with the Médoc. As there are no *grands crus classés* châteaux here, people pay the area little attention. This is a mistake.

The countryside of the northern Haut-Médoc is extremely attractive, with gently sloping hills and small, seemingly sleepy, picturesque villages – quite different from the rather flat terrain in the centre and south. And at the wine estates here you will meet generally hospitable growers, pleased to invite you in and offer a glass of wine. The pleasure is doubled if you buy a couple of bottles. Places to eat, however, can be few and far between. There are village inns where a sandwich or a simple dish will be prepared, but they do little more than just satisfy the hunger.

In general, connoisseurs rate wines from Saint-Seurin-de-Cadourne above those from Vertheuil, Saint-Sauveur and Cissac. Perhaps this is due to the soil and the situation, for Saint-Seurin is practically on the river. Geologically it is on an outlier of the Saint-Estèphe plateau and a certain relationship in the wines cannot be denied. Château Sociando-Mallet is one of the typical estates.

Vertheuil, between Cissac and Pez, is another attractive place to head for. Not only are there a couple of good châteaux, but the little village itself has an improbably large church: 11th-century Romanesque and 15th-century, as well as a fine ancient churchyard. Also, there is an abbey that is listed as a protected monument. Exhibitions are held here.

CISSAC

RECOMMENDED PRODUCERS

Château du Breuil
Cru Bourgeois
A beautiful estate where the château dates from 13th century.
Château Cissac
Cru Bourgeois
Tel: 56 59 58 13 or 56 59 58 39
An elegant wine.
Château Hanteillan
Cru Bourgeois (Hanteillan)
Tel: 56 59 35 31 Open every day.
Château Lamothe-Cissac
Cru Bourgeois
Tel: 56 59 58 16 Visits by appointment.

ST-SAUVEUR

RECOMMENDED PRODUCERS

Château Peyrabon
Cru Bourgeois Tel: 56 59 57 10
Well-made, good quality wine.
Château Ramage la Bâtisse
Cru Bourgeois Tel: 56 59 57 24
Well balanced, deep and complex.
Cooperative
The brand wine Canterayne.

Saint-Estèphe

----··----·-	Canton boundary
----····----	Commune (parish) bounda
CHÂTEAU	Cru Classé
Château	Cru Bourgeois
▨	Premier Cru Classé vineya
▨	Cru Classé vineyard
▢	Other vineyard
▨	Woods
═20═	Contour interval 10 metres
▨	Wine route

Left *In addition to being famous for its fine wines, St-Estèphe was also a busy port, once vying in importance with Bordeaux. All that now remains is a tiny harbour used mainly by fishing boats and yachts.*

SAINT-ESTEPHE

Travelling south from the tip of the Médoc, Saint-Estèphe is the first of the major wine communes that you will reach. Take the D204E3 east through the tiny village of Pez, and you will find yourself there. You have now left behind the fairly flat Médoc and entered a hillier, more romantic area – a region of distant views.

At practically every crossroad and junction in Saint-Estèphe there are signposts clearly showing how to get to the châteaux. And these signs are certainly needed, as all the small hills around here mean you often cannot see sufficiently far ahead and can easily lose your way.

Saint-Estèphe itself is a small village: the core of the commune, surrounded by many little hamlets. Cos (the 's' is pronounced) is one example, a '*lieu-dit*'. In terms of its actual vineyard area, Saint-Estèphe is the biggest of the six community appellations in the Médoc. But it has only five *grands crus classés* (not many compared to the others).There are a good number of *crus bourgeois*, however, and in recent years Saint-Estèphe wines have always been well placed in the competition for the Coupe des Crus Bourgeois.

Saint-Estèphe forms the geographical centre of the Médoc, equidistant from Pointe de Grave (57 kilometres

1:42,000

Km. 0   1   2 Km.
Miles 0   1 Mile

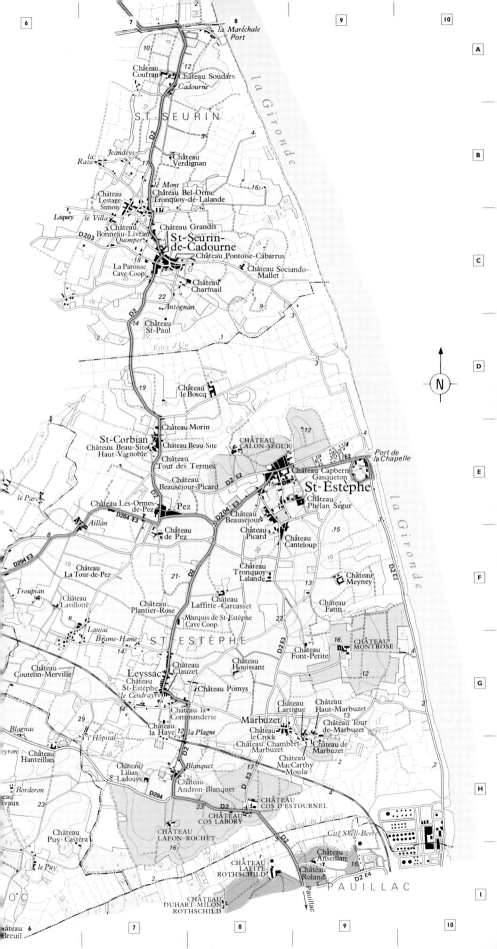

Far right *Château de Marbuzet, a striking Louis XVI building with a small vineyard. It is also the second wine of Cos d'Estournel.*
Main picture *Château Lilian-Ladouys, the commune's rising star. Christian and Liliane Thiéblot established the 50-hectare property in 1989.*
Below *Fresh vegetables fill the market stalls throughout the region.*

away) and Bordeaux. The soil shows all the typical Médoc characteristics: layers of limestone, plenty of gravel, and sometimes clay; and the slopes here are ideal for vines in terms of natural drainage and distribution of water. The presence of the Gironde can be sensed, and is directly visible too, in many places. Château Montrose even used to have its own landing stage.

The village of Saint-Estephe has a fine church with a distinctive tower – according to local inhabitants, this (appropriately enough) was built to resemble a wine bottle. There are other vinicultural stopping points, too. Opposite the church is the Maison du Vin, where there is an impressive collection of wines, sold at the normal prices – the firmer Saint-Estèphe wines are eminently suitable for keeping. And from 1st July to 15th September the Marquis de Saint-Estèphe (the local cooperative) is open to visitors, including weekends. It is a striking building standing beside the road and cannot be missed. If you want to eat, however, it is probably advisable to go on to Pauillac or Saint-Laurent.

ST-ESTEPHE

HOTEL

Château Pomys
Tel: 56 59 32 26
There are *chambres d'hôte* here from around FF250.

SPECIAL INTEREST

A very pleasant route leads from Porte de la Chapelle, St-Estèphe's somewhat reduced harbour, to Pauillac. This little-known road is attractive as it is one of the few places where you can view and photograph the vineyards from the riverside.

RECOMMENDED PRODUCERS

Château Calon-Ségur
Grand Cru Classé (3ème)
Tel: 56 59 30 08 or 56 59 30 27
In the 17th century this estate was the property of the rich and powerful Alexandre de Ségur, whose other possessions included châteaux Lafite, Latour, Mouton and de Pez. Château Calon was, however, his favourite. Keep this wine for five years at least before drinking.

Château Cos d'Estournel
Grand Cru Classé (2ème)
Tel: 56 73 15 55
One of the two stars of St-Estèphe. Intense, powerful, aromatic wine that keeps for some time. The d'Estournel

family had various properties in St-Estèphe in the 17th century, including a vineyard in the hamlet of Caux (the old spelling of Cos). 'Caux' proved in fact to be better than the other St-Estèphe vineyards, mainly because of the very gravelly slopes on which the vines were planted. Today the Plats family owns Cos d'Estournel, under whose management the château, modern winery and spacious cellar are perfectly maintained.

Château Le Crock
Cru Bourgeois
Tel: 56 59 30 33
Wine that has attracted great interest in recent years – and deservedly so.

Château Haut-Marbuzet
Cru Bourgeois
Tel: 56 59 30 54
Not to be confused with Château de Marbuzet, which is Cos d'Estournel's second wine. Haut-Marbuzet is a great wine with power and a deliciously complex finish.

Château La Haye
Cru Bourgeois (Leyssac)
Tel: 56 59 32 18
Legend has it this château was the runaway meeting point of Diane de Poitiers and King Henri II of France. The château dates from 1557 and the letters D and H, the initials of Diane and Henri, are carved in its stones. Deeply coloured, delicate wines.

Château Meyney
Cru Bourgeois
Tel: 56 31 44 44
Wine with more firmness than finesse.

Château Montrose
Grand Cru Classé (2ème)
Tel: 56 59 30 12
The second star in the St-Estèphe firmament. These wines are powerful, rich and harmonious. The estate is reminiscent of Alsace, keeping alive the memory of a former owner, Alsace-born Marthieu Dolfus, who acquired the château in 1866. There are still telling road signs on the estate – Rue d'Alsace, Rue de Mulhouse – although Montrose is now under the dynamic management of Jean-Louis Charmolüe.

Château les Ormes de Pez
Cru Bourgeois
Tel: 56 73 24 00
Visits by appointment.

Château Phélan-Ségur
Cru Bourgeois
Tel: 56 59 30 09
After heavy investments in the estate, the wines are, again, excellent.

Château Pomys
Cru Bourgeois (Leyssac)
Tel: 56 59 32 26
Substantial wines, but also supple, with a fine balance of oak and fruit.

ST-LAURENT MEDOC

HOTEL

La Rennaissance
Tel: 56 59 40 29
Simple village inn with ten rooms. A good place for a simple, tasty meal: set menus from around FF65. Many regional dishes, including *anguilles au vert* (eels in wine and herb sauce). The wine list is somewhat sparse. Very simple rooms from about FF180.

RECOMMENDED PRODUCERS

Château Balac
Cru Bourgeois
Sound wine with a pleasant finish.

Château Barateau
Cru Bourgeois
Tel: 56 59 42 07
Smooth, fruity wine.

Château Belgrave
Grand Cru Classé (5ème)
Tel (and Fax): 56 59 40 20
A *cinquième grand cru classé*. Totally renovated in 1979, and the quality of the wine is still improving.

Château Camensac
Grand Cru Classé (5ème)
Tel: 56 59 41 69
Visits by appointment.
Powerful wine with good length.

Above *The distinctive pagoda-like architecture of Cos d'Estournel, one of the commune's finest estates.*
Main picture *The Porte de la Chapelle, the tiny harbour on the Gironde at St-Estèphe. Until 1704, a much larger church overlooked it, the Nôtre Dame Entre-Deux-Arcs.*

SAINT-LAURENT-MEDOC

Saint-Laurent-Médoc is a true wine-growing community for there are no fewer than three *grands crus classés* here, and also some award-winning *crus bourgeois*. Yet it has no appellation of its own (as neighbouring Listrac and Moulis have) and growers are assigned to Haut-Médoc. In 1982, however, a *syndicat viticole* was set up, which is always the first condition required by the INAO (Institut National des Appellations d'Origine) for a district ultimately to acquire its own status.

Saint-Laurent is not on the D2 wine route but on the N215 *voie rapide*: the quickest link between Bordeaux and Pauillac. On an industrial estate beside the N215 is an imposing, gleaming 'wine factory', where the world's best-known brand wine, Mouton Cadet, is made and bottled.

Saint-Laurent's three *grands crus classés*, châteaux Belgrave, Camensac and La Tour Carnet, are situated on a sloping plateau that stretches towards Saint-Julien. Their wines therefore have much in common with those of Saint-Julien – it might almost have been more logical to admit Saint-Laurent Médoc into the Saint-Julien appellation.

Château Caronne Ste-Gemme
Cru Bourgeois
Sound wine with good colour, style and fruit character.

Château Larose-Trintaudon
Cru Bourgeois
Tel: 56 59 41 72
This is the Médoc's largest wine estate: it belongs to the French insurance company AGF and makes reliable wine.

Château La Tour Carnet
Grand Cru Classé (4ème)
Tel: 56 59 40 13 or 56 59 47 32 (chais)
A fourth growth *grand cru classé* producing charming, elegant wines to be drunk reasonably early.

Above *One of many ornate sculptures found on the estates throughout Bordeaux. This one stands in the grounds of Château Montrose in St-Estèphe.*

The Saint-Laurent plateau is fairly high and very susceptible to night frosts. In April 1991, for example, this led to a disaster in which 80 percent of the vines was affected by frost in a single night. At its western edge it is well-wooded and, with the one exception of Château de Cartujac, has no winegrowing. These woods are cherished as places to look for the famous *cèpes*, the *boletuses* (wild mushrooms) that taste so marvellous as a garnish for red meat. Saint-Laurent-Médoc itself has become a peaceful place since its bypass was built, and there is hardly any traffic in the centre of the village. It has an interesting church. A point worth noting in Saint-Laurent is that one of the smallest Médoc wine estates, Château le Bouscat, is situated here as well Château Larose-Trintaudon, the biggest of them all.

If you are travelling from Bordeaux and want to travel in the opposite direction, from Saint-Laurent to Saint-Estèphe, this is the route you should follow: first take the D206 and then bear left just before Pauillac, towards Saint-Estèphe. At the railway crossing in Pauillac you will get back on to the D2 again. Shortly after passing Château Lafite-Rothschild you cross the little Jalle de Breuil stream and, almost without noticing, you come to the Pauillac boundary. You then climb to the remarkable Cos d'Estournel with its pagoda towers. Bear right here and head past Lalande into Saint-Estèphe itself.

PAUILLAC

The Médoc has of course no capital in any legal sense, but many connoisseurs are of the opinion that, if there were to be one, the small town of Pauillac (population just under 6,000) would well merit this title. The big difference between the Pauillac appellation and the other wine communities is that its château names are more important than that of the commune itself. Professor Emile Peynaud once expressed it thus: 'Here the château provides the name and the fame'. This is well represented by the fact that there are 18 *grand cru* châteaux in total, and of the Médoc's four *premiers grands crus* three of them are from Pauillac. Even the cooperative has a more than merely good reputation, though its members are declining in number as the region's reputation more than enables each château to make and market its own wines.

This little harbour town on the River Gironde differs also in its history. The many surveys of the wine districts of the Médoc began with the coming of the Romans, but not so Pauillac's. Until the 14th century, the Bordeaux vineyards certainly extended no further north than Macau, reaching the Margaux area in the 15th century. It was only in the course of the 17th century that vineyard plantations spread any further north in the Médoc region. And winegrowing did not develop fully in the Pauillac area until later on in the 18th century, when the Bordeaux merchants first began to invest in it.

For hundreds of years the town of Pauillac had, however, benefited from its favourable situation on the

Pauillac

_ . _ . _	Canton boundary
_ . . _ . _	Commune (parish) boun...
CHÂTEAU	Cru Classé
Château	Cru Bourgeois
▨	Premier Cru Classé viney...
▧	Cru Classé vineyard
☐	Other vineyard
▣	Woods
—20—	Contour interval 10 metr...
▬▬▬	Wine route

Left The importance of wine to the Médoc, both culturally and economically, is reflected in sculptures and architecture.

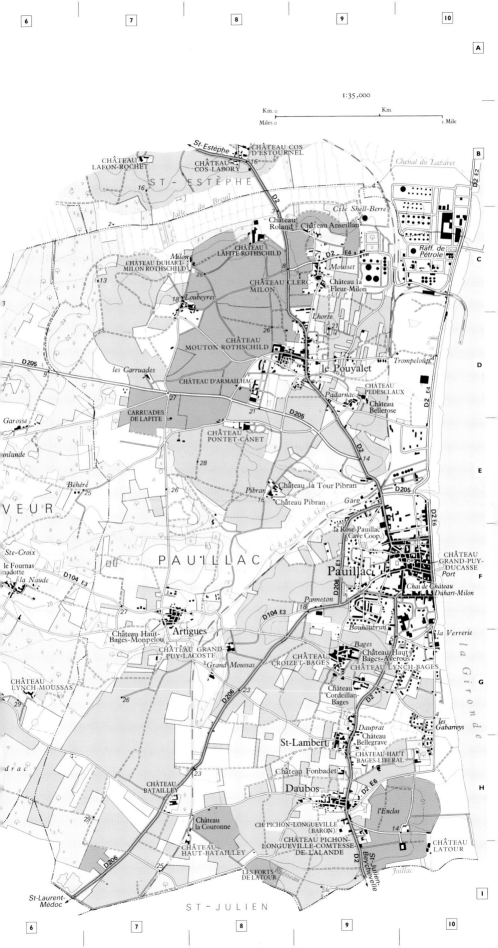

Above and right *Pauillac, the 'capital' of the Médoc, is a good place to stop off for shopping or simply to take a break from visiting châteaux.* Far right *Unlike the other major wine towns in the Médoc, Pauillac is situated directly on the Gironde.*

PAUILLAC

HOTELS

Château Cordeillan-Bages
Tel: 56 59 24 24
Excellent hotel/restaurant, a member of Relais & Châteaux. The rooms are luxurious, at prices from about FF700. Lounge and restaurant are most tastefully furnished. The quality of the cuisine is usually very good, with a distinct classic basis. The wine list is simply splendid, with all the famous Médoc names. Set menus start below FF200. Recommended: the lunch menu from around FF350, including wine and coffee.

Hôtel de France et Angleterre
Tel: 56 59 01 20
This quayside hotel-restaurant has been rebuilt and refurnished. Attractive rooms with modern furnishings, named after different châteaux: always ask for one at the back. Menus, from around FF100, of decent country cooking. Large wine list. All in all, a pleasant and affordable place to stay in the heart of the Médoc.

Gironde. The surrounding infrastructure was good and the larger sailing ships were able to take on full cargoes here. An added benefit of the port was the fact that it was a convenient sailing distance, of one tide, from both the Atlantic in one direction and the city of Bordeaux in the other. And because of this Pauillac was granted maritime rights in the Middle Ages, so foreign ships were obliged to take on board a pilot and four seamen from the town. Seafarers awaiting the turn of the tide stayed in Pauillac, and many a tavern undoubtedly did well out of this. Its docks were also used many times by boats sailing towards England to strengthen relationships between the two countries. The influential businessman Lafayette was particularly active in this respect, in the 1700s.

Today the yacht harbour is well known for its excellent facilities. The Maison du Vin stands right beside it, where the quay starts. Wines from many Pauillac châteaux can be

RESTAURANT

La Salamandre
Tel: 56 59 08 68
Simple place to eat on the quay, better known locally as 'Chez Johan'. Always busy at lunchtimes. Low-priced set menus, fish and other seafood dishes. Not bad; nothing out of the ordinary.

SPECIAL INTEREST

The annual Médoc marathon has a wine connection: the whole of this unique 42-km course runs through the vineyards, starting and finishing in Pauillac. A carnival mood prevails, giving the race a very special atmosphere. It is held mid-September.

RECOMMENDED PRODUCERS

Château d'Armailhac
Grand Cru Classé (5ème)
Tel: 56 59 22 22
The former Mouton-d'Armailhacq was bought in 1933 by Baron Philippe de Rothschild of Mouton Rothschild, the adjoining estate. From 1956 until 1974 the estate was called Mouton Baron Philippe; 'Baron' was changed to 'Baronne' in 1975 in honour of the Baron's late wife, Pauline. Since 1989, it has reverted to the original name: d'Armailhac. Alluringly aromatic wines with lovely juicy fruit.

Château Batailley
Grand Cru Classé (5ème)
Tel: 56 59 01 13 or 56 00 00 70
Visit this estate to see the park: the trees come from all over the world. Decent wine, with soft tannin, and a pleasant, fruity character.

Château Clerc Milon
Somewhat undervalued: a great and complex wine in recent years.

Château La Couronne
Subtle fruit characterizes this charming, stylish Pauillac. Delicious.

Château Duhart-Milon-Rothschild
Good, distinguished wine; hints of oak.

Château Fonbadet
Cru Bourgeois *Tel: 56 59 02 11*
Deeply-coloured, harmonious Pauillac.

Château Grand-Puy Ducasse
Grand Cru Classé (5ème)
Meaty, juicy, with lovely aromas of fruit and a fine touch of wood.

Château Grand-Puy Lacoste
Grand Cru Classé (5ème)
Tel: 56 59 06 66
Powerful, elegant, complex wine. There is a canal-side garden nearby.

Château Haut-Batailley
Grand Cru Classé (5ème)
Tel: 56 00 00 70 An unpretentious estate managed by Borie family. Well-rounded wine, with fruity length.

bought here at current prices, and you can obtain information about visiting them, and guided tours around them, too. Roughly in the middle of the waterfront boulevard stands the Château Grand Puy-Ducasse with its *chai* and *cuverie*. Its vineyards actually lie outside the town, and were originally pieced together from a number of different parcels of land during the 1740s.

The highly esteemed Château Mouton Rothschild has a unique and splendid wine museum set up by the late Baron Philippe de Rothschild and his wife. A visit here is an absolute must for any wine-lover. Visits and guided tours are arrangeable by appointment only (telephone 56 59 22 22), and take care to visit on the right day as the museum is closed at weekends, on public holidays, and throughout all of August.

Pauillac's winegrowing region consists of two parts, the little Chenal du Gaer stream, which flows into the Gironde behind the station, can be taken as the dividing line. This natural boundary results from the presence of two practically identical gravel plateaux. On the northern one there are the châteaux of Lafite-Rothschild, Mouton Rothschild and Pontet-Canet. Among the châteaux to the south, towards Saint-Julien, there are Château Latour, Château Lynch-Bages

Above *Work taking place amongst the vines at Château Pontet-Canet, neighbour of Château Mouton Rothschild in Pauillac.*

Right *Pauillac is famous for its milk-fed lamb, agneau de lait, which is wonderful served with the local wines.*

Far right *The splendid Château Mouton Rothschild.*

Château Lafite-Rothschild
Grand Cru Classé (1er)
Tel: 56 73 18 18
Baron Eric de Rothschild took over in 1980. Refined, subtley complex in aroma, palate and finish – one of the world's most stunning wines. The 18th-century château can't be visited but the splendid new cellars can.

Château Latour
Grand Cru Classé (1er)
Tel: 56 59 00 51
Derives its name from a former fortress on the site: the solitary domed tower in the grounds today is not the remains of a medieval fortification but a *pigeonnier*. A wine of superlatives: strong, intense and reliable – has been trumping its rivals for decades. Long bottle-ageing is essential.

Château Lynch-Bages
Grand Cru Classé (5ème)
Tel: 56 73 24 00
Great, classic Pauillac: red berry fruits dominate a harmonious palate. It far exceeds its 5ème *cru* classification.

Château Mouton Rothschild
Grand Cru Classé (1er in 1973)
Tel: 56 59 22 22 or 56 73 21 29
No other Bordeaux estate has had so much published about it, and no other *propriétaire* has been so much written about as the late Baron Philippe. When the management of Mouton passed to him in 1922 it was more of a farm

and the two Pichons. Château Latour is in the separate hamlet of Saint-Lambert, which used to be a part of the Saint-Julien commune.

Nowadays there is also white wine made in Pauillac. Lynch-Bages released one, Lynch Blanc, at the end of 1991. And at the beginning of 1993, Château Mouton Rothschild brought out another, Aile d'Argent, a white estate wine. These, of course, are not allowed full AC Pauillac status, and must be sold under the Bordeaux appellation, but there is talk of a Médoc Blanc category for the future. Up until 1956 there had been many châteaux producing white wine, but mostly for their own consumption. In February 1956, however, a hard frost destroyed a great many of the region's vines. In the subsequent replanting, white grape varieties were not even considered.

Today there is also great interest in the so-called 'second wines' of the *grands crus classés*. This must surely be the result of the higher demands being placed on the top estates. More stringent selection of the grapes at harvest means a higher proportion of the fruit is found not to be good enough for the *grand cru* itself – with the result that wine at the next level down benefits, gaining in power and style. Les Forts de Latour is often quoted as the most celebrated of these second wines. Strictly speaking, however, it is no longer a sec-

than a château. With great vision and tenacity, the Baron successfully made Mouton one of the most respected and visited wine estates in the world; and this despite the fact he was poet, playwright, film and theatre director and racing driver. With his American wife, Pauline, he created a unique wine museum, and since 1946 commissioned a work by a famous artist each year for the Mouton label. The Baron's greatest coup was the promotion of Mouton Rothschild in 1973 from first of the second-growths to its rightful place as a *premier cru* – the only change ever made to the 1855 classification. It is formidable, with a sumptuous cedarwood and red fruits and berries aroma.

Château Pibran
Cru Bourgeois
Racy and intense, with plenty of colour and tannin. A better *crus bourgeois*.

Château Pichon-Longueville
Grand Cru Classé (2ème)
Tel: 56 73 17 17
Turrets and steep-pitched roofs characterize this château. In 1990 it was completely renovated under the auspices of Jean-Michel Cazes and Axa-Millésimes. The new cellars are of striking design and the wine is better than ever: ripe fruit and oak ensure a firm yet smooth, elegant mouthful.

Château Pichon-Longueville, Comtesse de Lalande
Grand Cru Classé (2ème)
Tel: 56 59 19 40
A wine of impressive quality: rich in wood and fruit and always perfectly balanced. The Comtesse is the larger portion of what was once a single estate; the balance is Baron.

Château Pontet-Canet
Grand Cru Classé (5ème)
Tel: 56 59 04 04
The winery is enormous. The loft over the *cuvier* can seat up to 600 (for receptions) and the high-ceilinged cask cellar is quite cathedral-like. The wine is dark and concentrated with lots of fruit and a long finish.

ond wine but altogether a *cru* in its own right. Another renowned Pauillac second wine is the Carruades (formerly called Moulins de Carruades) from Lafite-Rothschild. Château Mouton Rothschild, on the other hand, has no second wine.

Pauillac's well-known cooperative has the euphonious name of La Rose Pauillac. It markets a Pauillac appellation wine under the same name. Visitors are welcome there six days of the week. You will find the cooperative near the railway station in the Rue du Maréchal Joffre.

And no wine-lover leaving Pauillac for Saint-Julien could ever simply drive past the new buildings at Château Pichon-Longueville Baron: in fact you pass between the *chais* on the D2. The château itself, which certainly deserves a visit, is 19th-century in style, but beside it are very modern winery and cellar structures, designed with great artistry. Pichon-Longueville Baron is a futuristic monument based on the 21st-century wine-drinker. Visitors are welcome on any day.

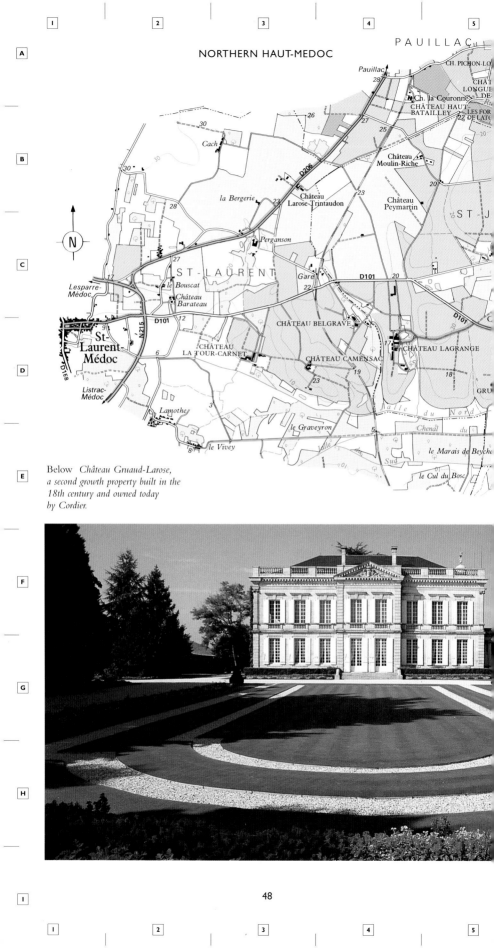

P A U I L L A C

CH. PICHON-LO

Pauillac
28

Ch. la Couronne
CHÂTEAU HAUT-
BATAILLEY

CHÂT
LONGUE
DE
LES FOR
DE LAT
22

25

26

27

30

Cach

Château
Moulin-Riche
20

la Bergerie
23

Château
Larose-Trintaudon
23

Château
Peymartin

S T - J

28

Perganson

27

ST-LAURENT

Gare
22

D101
20

Lesparre-
Médoc
17

le Bouscat

Château
Barateau

D101

D101

D101

St-
Laurent-
Médoc
9

N215

12

6

CHÂTEAU
LA TOUR-CARNET

CHÂTEAU BELGRAVE

CHÂTEAU CAMENSAC

CHÂTEAU LAGRANGE
17
18

19

23

GRU

Listrac-
Médoc

Lamothe
3

le Graveyron
5

Vallée du Nord

Chenal du

le Vivey
8

le Marais de Beyche

le Cul du Bosc

Sud

Below *Château Gruaud-Larose,*
a second growth property built in the
18th century and owned today
by Cordier.

Saint-Julien

—·····—·—	Canton boundary
—·········—	Commune (parish) boundary
CHÂTEAU	Cru Classé
Château	Cru Bourgeois
▨	Premier Cru Classé vineyard
▨	Cru Classé vineyard
▢	Other vineyard
▢♠	Woods
══20══	Contour interval 10 metres
▨	Wine route

1:42,000

Km. 0   1   2 Km.
Miles 0   1 Mile

SAINT-JULIEN-BEYCHEVELLE

The commune of Saint-Julien-Beychevelle consists of two nuclei: the village of Saint-Julien itself and the former Beychevelle. The two places have little to offer the visitor apart from their wines, around which everything here seems to revolve. Of the very greatest importance are the 11 *grands crus classés* châteaux. Producing these wines takes up 85 percent of the vineyard area – covering some 825 hectares. But there are quite a few other interesting châteaux to explore, too.

Approaching on the D2 from Pauillac, you will first reach Saint-Julien itself, with an interesting church as one of its key sights to see. The village – where the square is pleasant enough but serves no great purpose – is enclosed by the châteaux of the three Léovilles. The Marquis de Léoville's estate was originally one of the biggest in the Médoc until, after the Revolution, it was split into three: Léoville-las-Cases (the largest), Léoville-Poyferré and Léoville-Barton (the smallest). Although the other two Léovilles are of a high calibre, Léoville-las-Cases has had the most publicity in the last ten years. This is not surprising, for the owner's aim has been to compete with the *premiers grands crus classés*. He has been successful every year, with unfortunate consequences

ST-JULIEN-BEYCHEVELLE

RECOMMENDED PRODUCERS

Château Beychevelle
Grand Cru Classé (4ème)
Tel: 56 59 23 00
This 17th-century château is one of
the most beautiful in the Médoc. The
wine is intense and calls for patience
– the rewards are worth the wait.

Below *The fourth growth Château
St-Pierre.*

Château Branaire
Grand Cru Classé (4ème)
Tel: 56 59 25 86
Fine flowery aromas and elegant finish.
Château Ducru-Beaucaillou
Grand Cru Classé (2ème)
Tel: 56 59 05 20
Set majestically against the east
(riverside) slope of the more southerly
of the St-Julien gravel plateaux. The
façade, flanked by two stout Victorian
towers, looks towards the Gironde,
and a magnificent park enhances
the view. The wine is complex, and
perfectly balanced.
Château Gloria
Tel: 56 59 08 18
Balanced, generous wine.
Château Gruaud-Larose
Grand Cru Classé (2ème)
Tel: 56 31 44 44
One of the most finely tuned wines
from this village. The large château
with its Louis XVI salons and beautiful
park was totally renovated in 1995.

for the price of his wine. Less affluent enthusiasts find his
second wine, the Clos du Marquis, more accessible.
Léoville-las-Cases has in recent years certainly reached the
grand cru classé level.

The name of Henri Martin is indissolubly linked with
Saint-Julien. He was not only its *maire* and a grower, but also
one of the founders of the wine fraternity Commanderie du
Bontemps de Médoc et des Graves. Martin died in 1991 and
is commemorated by a bronze bust, which stands in a little
garden at Beychevelle, in the sharp bend in the D2 beside
Château Saint-Pierre – which belonged to Henri Martin.
(Just before this bend you will see a huge
wine bottle – this is a publicity stunt that
in fact looks rather vulgar.)

An interesting but little-known detail
here is that the three châteaux of
Beychevelle, Branaire, and Gruaud-Larose
were built in the 18th century in line with
one another. Château Beychevelle is the
most famous, especially for its imposing
frontage, and visitors should also take care
to look round the back too: there is a

Château Lagrange
Grand Cru Classé (3ème)
Tel: 56 59 23 63
This is one of the most interesting
Médoc châteaux to visit. Since it was
taken over by the Japanese drinks
giant Suntory towards the end of
1983, almost everything on this big
estate has been altered or renovated,
from the *cuvier* to the lookout tower.
The wine, classic St-Julien, is still
improving.

Château Lalande-Borie
Refined, well-structured wine with
plenty of fruit.

Château Langoa-Barton
Grand Cru Classé (3ème)
Tel: 56 59 06 05
One of the gems of the Médoc: a
chartreuse built above cellars, with a
lovely terraced garden behind. This is
the only *grand cru* still owned and
inhabited by the same family as in
1855, when the Classification was set
up. The wine itself is very like its big
brother, Léoville-Barton, but with
rather less depth.

Château Léoville-Barton
Grand Cru Classé (2ème)
For details see Langoa above
The smallest Léoville, owned by
the Barton family, who came from
Ireland early in the 18th century.
Deep-coloured, rich and powerfully-
structured wine.

Above *Barrels stacked in the cellar
of the 17th-century Château
Beychevelles.*
Main picture *This aeriel view of
Gruaud-Larose demonstrates how
dramatically the châteaux of the
Médoc stand out against the flat,
often dull landscape.*

Château Léoville-las-Cases
Grand Cru Classé (2ème)
Tel: 56 59 25 26
After the French Revolution the estate of the Marquis de Léoville was split into three: the present châteaux Léoville-las-Cases (the largest), Léoville-Poyferré and Léoville-Barton. Perfectionist Michel Delon produces a memorable wine, rather tough when young, but developing aristocratic quality with time.
Château Léoville-Poyferré
Grand Cru Classé (2ème)
Tel: 56 59 08 30
Still a little undervalued, but deserves its second growth status for its pure breeding, fruit, and length of aftertaste.
Château Moulin de la Rose
Tel: 56 59 08 45
Excellent wine, rich in colour, with a respectable amount of tannin.

superb view of the River Gironde from this château. Beychevelle formerly belonged to the dukes of Epernon. One of them was an Admiral of France and the story goes that seamen coming up the River Gironde had to show due respect to the admiral by lowering the sails of their boats when they came in sight of his château – hence its name. In the Gascon vernacular the expression was *bacha velo*, in other words, *baisser la voile*, 'lower the sails'. Evidently they still appreciate such courtesies in Saint-Julien, for the visitor crossing the commune boundary will read a sign saying '*passants, vous entrez dans le très célèbre et très illustre cru de Saint-Julien. Saluez*'.

At Château Branaire an impressive *chai* has been built with a laboratory-like tasting area in its centre. And between châteaux Beychevelle and Saint-Laurent lies the large estate of Château Lagrange which, since 1983, has belonged to the Japanese drinks giant, Suntory. Practically everything on this estate, from the buildings to the vineyards, has been rebuilt, renewed, revitalised or refurbished, and it is now one of the finest properties in the Médoc – and one that's well worth the visit if you have time. With all the subsidiary buildings nearby, the château rather resembles a small 19th-century village.

Above *Léoville-Poyferré, one of the three Léovilles comprising the Marquis de Léoville's estate which was broken up in 1789.*
Right *Château Beychevelle. Built in the 17th century, the château is regarded as one of the most beautiful in the Médoc.*
Far right *Traditional gates hide high-technology at Château Lagune, owned by Champagne Ayala.*

Château St-Pierre
Grand Cru Classé (4ème)
Tel: 56 59 08 18
Rounded, approachable wine. Quality is still improving.
Château Talbot
Grand Cru Classé (4ème)
Tel: 56 73 21 50
With more than 100ha of vines, this is the largest property in St-Julien. It is named after John Talbot, Earl of Shrewsbury, who lodged here in 1453 before dying in battle with the French at Castillon. Attractive, noble wine with charm and good structure.

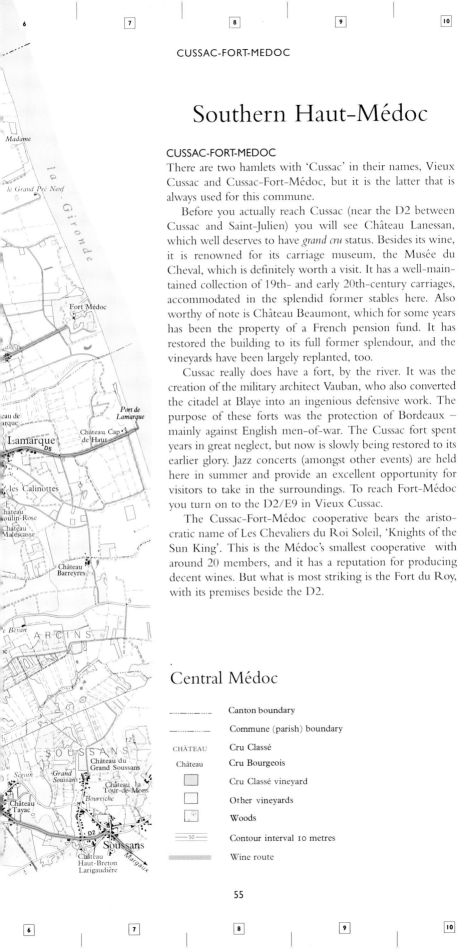

Southern Haut-Médoc

CUSSAC-FORT-MEDOC

There are two hamlets with 'Cussac' in their names, Vieux Cussac and Cussac-Fort-Médoc, but it is the latter that is always used for this commune.

Before you actually reach Cussac (near the D2 between Cussac and Saint-Julien) you will see Château Lanessan, which well deserves to have *grand cru* status. Besides its wine, it is renowned for its carriage museum, the Musée du Cheval, which is definitely worth a visit. It has a well-maintained collection of 19th- and early 20th-century carriages, accommodated in the splendid former stables here. Also worthy of note is Château Beaumont, which for some years has been the property of a French pension fund. It has restored the building to its full former splendour, and the vineyards have been largely replanted, too.

Cussac really does have a fort, by the river. It was the creation of the military architect Vauban, who also converted the citadel at Blaye into an ingenious defensive work. The purpose of these forts was the protection of Bordeaux – mainly against English men-of-war. The Cussac fort spent years in great neglect, but now is slowly being restored to its earlier glory. Jazz concerts (amongst other events) are held here in summer and provide an excellent opportunity for visitors to take in the surroundings. To reach Fort-Médoc you turn on to the D2/E9 in Vieux Cussac.

The Cussac-Fort-Médoc cooperative bears the aristocratic name of Les Chevaliers du Roi Soleil, 'Knights of the Sun King'. This is the Médoc's smallest cooperative with around 20 members, and it has a reputation for producing decent wines. But what is most striking is the Fort du Roy, with its premises beside the D2.

Central Médoc

·--·--·--·--	Canton boundary
·---------	Commune (parish) boundary
CHÂTEAU	Cru Classé
Château	Cru Bourgeois
▨	Cru Classé vineyard
☐	Other vineyards
☐	Woods
═ 50 ═	Contour interval 10 metres
▬▬▬	Wine route

Right and below right *Images from around the historical town of Lamarque: an old inscription on a wall and the Château de Lamarque, a preserved medieval fortress.*

CUSSAC-FORT-MÉDOC

RECOMMENDED PRODUCERS

Château Beaumont
Cru Bourgeois *Tel: 56 58 92 29*
Elegant wine with a lingering hint of blackcurrants and oak. Much new planting should give more depth.

Château Lachesnaye
Haut-Médoc that is elegant and yet firm, juicy and well-balanced. Same owner as Château Lanessan.

Château Lanessan
Cru Bourgeois Supérieur
Tel: 56 58 94 80
One of the very best Haut-Médocs, intense in taste, rich in tannin and with great potential for ageing. Also has a carriage museum.

Château du Moulin Rouge
Cru Bourgeois *Tel: 56 58 91 13*
Big, powerful wines.

Château Tour-du-Haut-Moulin
Cru Bourgeois
Tel: 56 58 91 10
A great wine with a rich, powerful length and supple tannins. Visitors are welcomed in the small château; the cellars are on the road to the fort.

LAMARQUE

RESTAURANT

Relais du Médoc
Tel: 56 58 92 27
Friendly local restaurant with good, appetizing food. Classic regional dishes. Set menus from below FF100, and a more expensive *menu Médocain* (including wine). There are a few simple rooms here at less than FF200.

L'Escale
Tel: 56 58 92 21
Next to the spot where the ferry leaves for Blaye. Simple, inexpensive. Emphasis on *fruits de mer.* Also a bar.

RECOMMENDED PRODUCERS

Château du Cartillon
Cru Bourgeois
Pleasant, elegant wine; firm structure.

Château de Lamarque
Cru Bourgeois
Tel: 56 58 90 03 or 56 58 97 55
Beautiful castle, immaculately maintained. The wines are nice too: strikingly smooth, often velvety Haut-Médoc with a firm core. The Réserve des Marquis d'Evry is even better.

LAMARQUE

The little village of Lamarque owes its reputation to water and to wine. Its connection with water is the ferry that links it with Blaye on the opposite bank of the Gironde. The wine element is given impressive form in Château de Lamarque.

The château was originally built as a fortress against attacks from the Gironde; you can reach it by way of a tree-lined drive. Parts of it are 11th- and 12th-century (the cellars and chapel), but the main structure dates from around the 14th. Inside there is a great hall with portrait paintings and fabulous antique furniture. The inner courtyard is beautiful too. Both the Duke of Gloucester and the French King Henry IV have lived there. Today it is the heart of a top wine estate.

From the little harbour at Lamarque there is a fine view across the water to the right bank of the Gironde.

On the way to Arcins you pass Château Maucaillou, with an interesting museum: the Musée des Arts et Métiers de la Vigne et du Vin. All stages of growing and making wine are displayed, together with a most ingenious 'scent organ', with which you can smell the different fragrances of wine.

ARCINS

However minuscule this village may be, there are good reasons for stopping here, namely the châteaux and a charming restaurant. Arcins is situated just outside the Margaux appellation on the D2. The wines are given the Haut-Médoc appellation, but they are in fact very like those of Margaux.

The region has a turbulent history. Although Château d'Arcins, for example, was producing 140,000 litres of wine a year in 1850, the arrival of phylloxera wrought such havoc that this scale of production fell drastically. Many wine estates fell into decay. Even as recently as a generation ago there were hardly any vineyards remaining at all. Increasing prosperity fortunately brought a turnaround, and investing in this former 'no man's land' became fashionable again. Châteaux Arnauld and d'Arcins represent this well, having been totally renewed and updated – both are open to visitors.

MOULIS

To get to Moulis you turn right in Arcins where the sign points to Château Chasse-Spleen. This route takes you to the famous Poujeaux plateau. If you turn left south of Grand Poujeaux the road brings you to the actual village of Moulis.

This is the smallest village appellation. Winegrowing began here in the Middle Ages on a purely ecclesiastical basis. Moulis was the second religious centre of the region after Bordeaux, with four priories and 34 parishes, and was therefore an important supplier of communion wine. In fact the Moulis legend tells of how a pope commissioned the building of two identical churches, one in Rome and the other in Moulis. The church completed first would become the centre of the whole Catholic faith. Moulis did not stand a chance. In a more concrete form there remains a beautiful Romanesque church here with fine statuary and carving, within and without.

Both 'Moulis' and 'Moulis-en-Médoc' are used as wine appellations – Moulis is more usual. Moulis' total vineyard area is 550 hectares, with the gravel of the Poujeaux plateau in the east, clay soils with lime in the northwest.

There are no *grands crus classés* in Moulis, but over the years some of its wines – notably

Château Malescasse
Cru Bourgeois
Tel: 56 58 90 09
Worth visiting.

ARCINS

RESTAURANT

Le Lion d'Or
Tel: 56 58 96 79
One of the best places to eat in the whole Médoc, with even an international reputation. Besides the main menu, owner and chef Barrier still keeps the simple lunchtime *menu familiale* at something below FF100. *Plats du jour* are written on a board beside the road outside. Good wines.

RECOMMENDED PRODUCERS
Château d'Arcins
Tel: 56 58 91 29
Has grown from 10 to 90ha in 15 years.
Château Arnauld
Cru Bourgeois
Tel: 57 88 50 34
An elegant, meaty, supple wine.

Château Tramont
Good, well-made wine; small estate.

MOULIS

HOTELS
CASTELNAU-DE-MEDOC
Restaurant-hôtel des Landes
Tel: 56 58 73 80
Simple village hotel where the cooking is good and where wine-buyers quite often stay. Rooms from a little under FF200. Set menus start below FF100.
Château Biston
Tel: 56 58 22 13
Good *chambres d'hôte*. Open March to November; costs around FF300.

those of châteaux Chasse-Spleen, Gressier Grand Poujeaux, Poujeaux and Maucaillou – have been ranged alongside the greatest of Bordeaux. Prices from these châteaux are generally higher than those from the rest of the village.

After the 1855 classification it was expected that Moulis wines would gradually win places amongst the classed growths. And in 1866 the local lawyer Bigeat wrote to the effect that the classification of a Moulis *cru* was only a matter of time. He could hardly have anticipated that practically nothing would ever change regarding the 1855 scheme.

LISTRAC-MEDOC

Listrac-Médoc, on the N215 (as with Moulis) has no *grand cru classé* châteaux, but it does have a communal appellation. As well as for some very celebrated châteaux, it is especially renowned for its energetically managed cooperative. Cave de Vinification de Listrac-Médoc, to use its official name, started in 1935 as a *cuverie* with a 5,000-hectolitre capacity – enormous in those days. Since 1948 the wine has gained quite a reputation being sold on French railways. Today, its capacity is nearly 30,000 hectolitres.

Within the commune boundaries here there are three famous small gravel hills: at Fonréaud, Fourcas and Listrac itself. Listrac's reaches a height of 43 metres, making it the Médoc's highest point – there is a fire tower perched there. Listrac's subsoil is further made up of layers of clay, lime and

gravel. For many years Merlot was the most important grape variety to grow on it, but at most wine estates you now find at least 50 percent Cabernet Sauvignon. This has overall increased the finesse of the wines. Listracs used to have a rather negative, rustic image. That has now changed, but they are still virile, firm structured, very substantial wines. A pleasant white wine is now made at Château Fonréaud, the only Listrac estate to do so.

The village itself clusters around a small 13th-century church with an interesting spire. The original name, Listrac, was altered to Listrac-Médoc in 1986 to avoid possible confusion with Lirac in the Rhône region.

LISTRAC-MEDOC

HOTEL

Château Cap Léon Veyrin
Tel: 56 58 07 28
Rooms and *table d'hôte* meals are available at this wine estate, but have to be booked. Prices of rooms from FF280.

RESTAURANT

Château Rose Ste-Croix
Tel: 56 58 08 68
Small, simple restaurant, run by a winegrower's family. Regional specialities. The cheapest menu is under FF100. Some *chambres d'hôte*.

RECOMMENDED PRODUCERS

Château Bellegrave
Tel: 56 58 02 40
Visits by appointment.
Château Cap Léon Veyrin
Tel: 56 58 07 28
Visits by appointment.
Château Clarke
Tel: 56 88 88 00
Created by Baron Edmund de Rothschild.
Château Fonréaud
Cru Bourgeois
Tel: 56 58 02 43
Collection of antique wine utensils on show.
Château Fourcas-Dupré
Cru Bourgeois
Tel: 56 58 01 07
Château Fourcas-Hosten
Cru Bourgeois
Tel: 56 58 01 15
Château Fourcas-Loubaney
Moulin de Laborde (Listrac-Médoc)
Tel: 56 58 03 83
Visits by appointment.
Château Lestage
Cru Bourgeois
Tel: 56 58 02 43
Visits by appointment.
Château Mayne-Lalande
Tel: 56 58 27 63
Modern, pleasant cellars.
Château Peyredon Lagravette
Cru Bourgeois
Tel: 56 58 05 55
Open every day except Sunday.

Above *Grape-pickers make their way to the vineyards. The Médoc harvest usually takes place during September.*
Left *The largest property in Moulis, Château Mauvesin, was built in 1853 by the Le Blanc family, which had owned the property since the mid-1600s.*

MARGAUX

To get to Margaux from Moulis there is a choice of routes: you can either drive via the D105 or return to the D2 at Arcins and approach this classic vineyard area on the wandering wine route. Between Margaux and Moulis is the little village of Avensan. It belongs to Haut-Médoc, but makes wines closely resembling those of Margaux. There are two interesting châteaux here: Citran and de Villegeorge.

Within the Margaux appellation itself there are about 1,250 hectares of vineyard. They cover four different communes: firstly, Margaux itself, then Soussans, Cantenac and Arsac. The vineyards may be disparate, but they do not spread as far as to include those mid-stream in the Gironde (opposite Margaux there are some islands in the river which also have vineyards). These are outside the Margaux appellation and their wines must be classified as Bordeaux and Bordeaux Supérieur.

The 1855 classification ascribed 21 *grands crus* to Margaux – more than to any other Médoc appellation. Also, all five

Above *Vines belonging to Château d'Issan in the commune of Cantenac* *in Margaux. Cantenac's vineyards are sited on gravel plateaux.*

Margaux

–·–·–·–	Canton boundary
–·–·–·–	Commune (parish) boundar
CHÂTEAU	Cru Classé
Château	Cru Bourgeois
▨	Premier Cru Classé vineya
▨	Cru Classé vineyard
☐	Other vineyard
⌂	Woods
══25══	Contour interval 5 metres
▬▬▬	Wine route

Right *A scenic corner of Château Cantemerle in the Macau commune of Margaux. This fifth growth property is now producing exemplary wines since a change of ownership in 1980.*

MARGAUX

 RESTAURANTS

Auberge de Savoie
Tel: 56 88 31 76
Congenial restaurant well-known for its very good value. Classic décor gives a pleasant atmosphere, too. Regional cuisine with modern presentation. The *quiche au foie de canard et jus de truffe* is delightful. Set menus.

Relais de Margaux
Tel: 56 88 38 20
Don't be deterred by the luxurious surroundings, you can eat excellently and at reasonable prices – sometimes in the company of château owners. Jazz brunches arranged on summer Sundays. There are luxurious rooms from FF750. Japanese proprietor.

 RECOMMENDED PRODUCERS

AVENSAN
Château Citran
Cru Bourgeois
Tel: 56 58 21 01
Much recent investment. A rich, harmonious Haut-Médoc with a complex, fruity, lingering aftertaste.

Château de Villegeorge
Cru Bourgeois
Tel: 57 88 70 20
Broad, deep-coloured wine with fruity overtones and length. Ageing potential.

MARGAUX
Château Margaux
Grand Cru Classé (1er)
Tel: 57 88 70 28
The most impressive château in the Médoc; an avenue lined with plane trees leads up to a huge country house. A masterly wine, one of the greatest in the world. Year in, year out it is of a magnificent quality, very concentrated, wonderfully complex. The second wine, Pavillon Rouge, merits recommendation, as does white Pavillon Blanc.

Château La Gurgue
Revitalised by the late Bernadette Villars. Recently wines have lightly spicy, fruity style and less oak.

Château Larruau
Tiny, serious estate. Charmingly fragrant wine with distinct tannin.

classes are represented in Margaux, which again is not an accolade awarded anywhere else. Such high quality in these wines is widely thought due to the fine composition of the soil. In Margaux this consists mainly of gravel brought down from the Massif Central and the Pyrenees in the Tertiary period. The soil is poorer than in other wine villages here. But poor soil usually gives a rich wine. The actual topsoil is thinner than elsewhere in the Médoc, the gravel content the highest, the microclimate the warmest, and production per hectare the lowest. In critiques, words such as 'elegant', 'feminine', 'subtle' and 'finesse' are used in describing Margaux's wines. These are not wines that reveal themselves quickly; you have to wait patiently before you can enjoy them. The rule of thumb is that a Margaux needs seven years before its qualities show to full advantage. But there are also firm, sturdier wines made here that demand even more

time. They come mostly from vineyards in the west of the area, where the soil has rather more clay.

The most northerly village in the Margaux group is Soussans. Not far from its centre is the site of Château La Tour de Mons, a mighty castle. It was largely destroyed by fire in 1895, and only the remains of towers, a chapel and stables (now a cellar for bottles) still stand today.

Margaux itself is next on the route and is one of the world's best-known wine names, in part because of Château Margaux. This building, erected in 1815, has the aura of a palace and is immaculately maintained. And in its cellars – they are partly underground, which is not common in the Médoc – sublime wine is matured. Just to the side of the impressive château's drive stands Margaux's church, dating from the 18th century.

The D2 makes a rather sudden left-angled turn into the village centre. At the end of the street you will see the Maison du Vin, where the fullest information about the appellation can be obtained. There is also a large assortment of wines on sale. At Sprengnether's, the local *pâtissier*, the famous *Sarments du Médoc* are made – little chocolate vine branches. Near the railway crossing, on the Arsac road, there is a small factory making wine cases. The lids of these cases marked with the château insignia make quite collectable items.

Leaving Margaux on the D2 travelling south, the next commune in the group is Cantenac. At its centre

Château Lascombes
Grand Cru Classé (2ème)
Tel: 56 88 70 66
Excellently managed estate (one of the Médoc's largest) with a rather ungainly 19th-century château. Firm, elegant Margaux that develops well in bottle.

Château Malescot St-Exupéry
Grand Cru Classé (3ème)
Tel: 57 88 70 68
Comfortable château, dating from 1885. Its scattered vineyards (some of them in Soussans) make balanced wine with colour, firmness, wood, and refinement. Needs patience.

Château Marquis d'Alesme Becker
Grand Cru Classé (3ème)
Tel: 57 88 70 27
Elegant, strong wine with supple tannin.

Château Marquis de Terme
Grand Cru Classé (4ème)
Tel: 57 88 30 01
During the 1980s a great deal has been invested in equipment, cellars and reception rooms. The wine has benefited; it is firmly structured with deep colour, good fruit and tannin.

Château Rausan-Ségla
Grand Cru Classé (2ème)
Tel: 57 88 70 30
Older than most Médoc estates, the Rausan vineyards date back to 1661. Since the 1980s, distinguished wine.

SOUSSANS
Château Labégorce
Cru Bourgeois
Tel: 57 88 71 32
Recently renovated and revitalised. The result – an engaging wine full of fruit and rather fat.

Château Labégorce Zédé
Tel: 56 88 71 31
Firm, award-winning, characterful, sound-structured wine; closed at first.

Above left *The peaceful village of Margaux.*
Left *A weathered statue in the grounds of Château Prieuré-Lichine.*

Château Tayac
Cru Bourgeois
Tel: 57 88 33 06
Pleasing wine with smooth fruity flavour.
Château La Tour de Bessan
Attractive wine: elegant without being truly refined. Mainly from Cabernet Sauvignon (rare in Margaux).
Château La Tour de Mons
Cru Bourgeois
Tel: 57 88 33 03
Estate with remains of a 13th-century castle. Deep-coloured wine, well-nigh inaccessible in youth, but develops well in bottle; has fruit, tannin, and a complex, long finish.

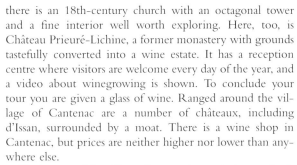

CANTENAC
Château d'Angludet
Cru Bourgeois
Tel: 57 88 71 41
Sichel family makes a wine that shines, with rich, complex aromas and taste.
Château Brane-Cantenac
Grand Cru Classé (2ème)
Tel: 57 88 70 20
Large, well-run Lurton property with prime vineyards on Cantenac's plateau. Quality levels vary, but fruity and elegant wines, good for ageing.
Château Cantenac-Brown
Grand Cru Classé (3ème)
Tel: 57 88 30 07
Imposing building. Powerful, well-balanced wine.
Château Desmirail
Grand Cru Classé (3ème)
Tel: 57 88 34 33
The Brane-Cantenac team makes the wine, now back on the scene. Today, it is a stylish wine with great finesse.
Château d'Issan
Grand Cru Classé (3ème)
Tel: 57 88 35 91 or 56 44 94 45
17th-century moated château; one of the most splendid sights in the Médoc. The wine is elegant with lovely aromas of red berry fruit and supple tannins.

there is an 18th-century church with an octagonal tower and a fine interior well worth exploring. Here, too, is Château Prieuré-Lichine, a former monastery with grounds tastefully converted into a wine estate. It has a reception centre where visitors are welcome every day of the year, and a video about winegrowing is shown. To conclude your tour you are given a glass of wine. Ranged around the village of Cantenac are a number of châteaux, including d'Issan, surrounded by a moat. There is a wine shop in Cantenac, but prices are neither higher nor lower than anywhere else.

To the east of the village, Cantenac's gravel plateaux leads on to pastures and watermeadows, or *palus*. Further away there is the tiny settlement of Labarde, where the D209 and D2 roads intersect near a railway crossing. Labarde belongs to the Margaux appellation. It has an 18th-century church housing a carved wooden main altar. Just outside it is Château Giscours, which is not only as a wine estate but also the headquarters of the Bordeaux polo club. Visitors can watch polo games every weekend in September.

Westwards from Cantenac, a narrow road winds through vineyards and woods towards minuscule Arsac – the southernmost

Margaux commune. On a low hill just outside this village stands the grey, angular Château du Tertre, a fifth growth *grand cru classé*. Château d'Arsac, on the other hand, has perhaps the most unorthodox frontage of any in the Médoc: all its wooden window frames and doors are painted a light blue colour. The building is impressively set in a fine park. The winemaking equipment here is modern, and there is a visitors' centre with exhibitions of modern art, which is open daily.

Château Kirwan
Grand Cru Classé ((3ème)
Tel: 56 81 24 10 or 57 88 71 42
An 18th-century manor house with a beautiful show of flowers in summer. Elegant wine with potential to mature.

Château Palmer
Grand Cru Classé (3ème)
Tel: 57 88 72 72
Picture-book château with its four pointed towers. Among the very best Médoc wines: stylish suppleness, great refinement and perfect balance.

Château Prieuré-Lichine
Grand Cru Classé (4ème)
Tel: 57 88 36 28
Probably the most hospitable Grand Cru in the Médoc. Former monastery. Today, the wine is well-balanced, and fairly elegant with decent tannin. Gains in richness and class in classic years.

ARSAC

Château d'Arsac
Tel: 56 58 83 90
Hospitable, dynamic, modern estate: cellars in striking blue. Art exhibitions.

Château Ligondras
Tel: 56 58 80 98 or 56 58 81 25
Robust, deep-coloured wine. Reliable.

Château Monbrison
Cru Bourgeois
Tel: 56 58 80 04
Exceptional wine: distinctive aroma and a full, exquisite, powerful length.

Château du Tertre
Carefully restored building on a low hill. The only *grand cru classé* here: excellent, elegant Margaux.

LABARDE

Château Dauzac
Grand Cru Classé ((5ème)
Tel: 57 88 32 10
Almost total renewal and renovation has led to a quality wine with plenty of aromas and complex, elegant length.

Château Giscours
Grand Cru Classé (3ème)
Tel: 57 97 09 09
Huge rambling château and *chais* in a fine park. Reliable wine with an intense palate, fine colour, and lingering tannin.

Above *Fertilizing and spraying in the vineyard are carried out judiciously, using preparations which are as natural as possible.*
Left *The imposing moated third growth Château d'Issan is one of the most spectacular sights in the Médoc.*
Far left *First growth Château Margaux, a beautiful country house.*

Château Siran
Tel: 57 88 34 04
Wines maturing in the nuclear-proof cellar here are charmingly rounded, full of finesse and pedigree.

MACAU

RESTAURANTS

Chez Quinquin
Tel: 57 88 45 89
On a terrace by the Gironde, this is a good, inexpensive place specializing in fish dishes. Attractive view over river.
La Guinguette
Tel: 56 30 08 12
Next to Chez Quinquin. Lots of *fruits de mer*. Sunday lunch for about FF130.

RECOMMENDED PRODUCERS

Château Cambon La Pelouse
Cru Bourgeois
Tel: 57 88 40 32
Charming wine with length; usually drinkable within two years of vintage.
Château Cantemerle
Grand Cru Classé (5ème)
Tel: 57 97 02 82
Fairy-tale château hidden in romantic woods. Very good wine since 1980s: concentrated, complex, rich in tannin.

Château Lescalle
Bordeaux Supérieur
Rounded taste of bilberries and supple tannin. Has potential for keeping.
Château Maucamps
Cru Bourgeois
Tel: 57 88 07 64
Very good wine with a growing reputation; elegant and pure.

LUDON

HOTEL

Not in fact an hotel, but an exceptionally good place to stay, is Madame de St-Paul, *chambres d'hôte*. Price for a room is just under FF200.

MACAU

From Labarde you can drive via the D209 or the D2 to Macau. Macau is a village with some 2,600 inhabitants. It also has a partly Romanesque church with a fine belltower. Apart from this it is hardly worth a visit; but in the immediate neighbourhood there are a few places that for various reasons merit a small detour. The first of these is on the D2, the fifth growth *grand cru classé* Château Cantemerle, with perhaps the finest set of railings in the whole Médoc. They enclose an impressive park. Just outside the village, near the Ludon road, is Château Maucamps, a large estate of nearly 60 hectares – about 15 hectares of it vineyard. This produces a Haut-Médoc wine with a reputation that has been growing steadily since 1981; the number of medals won at the various French wine *concours* is mounting up nicely.

Macau's little harbour on the Gironde used to be worthy of note; but although the signboard saying 'Port' is a reminder of this, decline has clearly set in. Near the water there is a pleasant *guinguette*, a small tavern and garden, that is a lovely spot to spend a relaxing few hours – especially in

summer, and certainly for lunch, when simple and good-tasting fish dishes are on the menu. From the harbour, a road runs south along an embankment, with vineyards to the right. Among them are those of Château Lescalle, which has the same owner as Château Maucamps. Château Lescalle, however, is not entitled to the Haut-Médoc appellation and is a Bordeaux Supérieur.

LUDON

From Macau it is just a short drive to Ludon, a little to the south. Ludon itself is a sleepy commuters' village, around a church built in various styles. An interesting collection of old winemaking equipment can be seen at Château d'Arche in the centre. Close to the D2 heading out of Ludon is Château La Lagune, the southernmost *grand cru classé* in the Médoc. The road there, which runs parallel to the D2, leads past Ludon's most important place of interest, Château d'Agassac. This is a weathered castle built in the 13th century on the foundations of an earlier feudal stronghold. The *seigneur* of Agassac was a thriftless gentleman who became involved in a scandal: one morning a servant was found dead in the château's moat. The *seigneur* was regarded as responsible but the whole affair was covered up. In the 16th century the castle passed into the hands of the Pomiès, a family which produced some well-known political figures. The present owners are the Capbern-Gasqueton family.

Above *Part of the immense Landes forest near Lac de Lacenau, just west of the Médoc.*
Above left *The Lion d'Or in Arcins, one of the most popular restaurants in the Médoc.*
Far left *Barrel-making in the village of Ludon, near Margaux.*

RESTAURANT

Le Petit Bacalan
Tel: 56 30 32 11
Country cuisine in an unpretentious setting. Reasonable prices.

RECOMMENDED PRODUCERS

Château d'Agassac
Cru Bourgeois
Stylish, concentrated, complete wine with an aftertaste rich in tannin.
Château Lafite-Canteloup
Tel: 56 35 05 36
Charming wine, drinkable two years after vintage.
Château La Lagune
Tel: 57 88 44 07
The 1730 château was originally a Carthusian monastery. Reliable, firm wine: well-balanced, mellow firmness, with a hint of vanilla from new casks.

SOUTHERN HAUT-MEDOC

RECOMMENDED PRODUCERS

Château Clément-Pichon
Cru Bourgeois
Tel: 56 35 23 79
Since 1977 wine has once again been made here with great success after the estate had lain fallow for nearly 60 years. A good Haut-Médoc with traces of new wood in its aftertaste.

Château Dillon
Cru Bourgeois
Blanquefort 33290
Tel: 56 35 56 35
The wine from the local agricultural school; easy to drink and showing typical characteristics. Exhibition of Erik Dietmann's 'Les gardiens des barriques' (large noses) is on permanent display.

Above *In contrast to the grandeur of the Bordeaux châteaux, a simple village home in Haut-Médoc.*
Below *The Abbey at La Réole (Entre-Deux-Mers).*

HAUT-MEDOC: THE SOUTHERN EXTREME

As you drive south from Ludon you head towards the end of the classic Médoc wine route. One of the last places you will come to is Parempuyre (just east of the D2) – despite its location it is still well worth the visit. It has a 19th-century church with paintings of the same period. One of Bordeaux's biggest wine firms is established in the village: CVBG, which belongs to the Dutch group Bols-Wessanen. Next to it is the entrance to the wholly restored Château Clément-Pichon; the drive cuts through the vineyard.

Next you will reach Blanquefort. Like most places on the outskirts of Bordeaux, Blanquefort consists of a jumble of

dwellings in every possible style. According to legend, the local castle (with a moat, six towers and a keep) is protected by the ghost of the Black Prince. In Blanquefort there is a school of agriculture and winegrowing (*lycée agricole*), which runs Château Dillon, its own estate. In the well-designed *chai* there is a permanent exhibition of 21 large 'noses'. This collection was bought by the French Ministry of Culture and then loaned to the school.

Above *The pier at Hourtin. The coast is just a few kilometres away from most Bordeaux vineyards.*
Left *Fruit on display in one of the local markets. Try serving fresh fruit such as melon with a glass of young Sauternes or Barsac.*

Château Magnol
Cru Bourgeois
Belongs to the large wine firm, Barton & Guestier, and makes an outstanding Haut-Médoc with power and depth.

Château du Taillan
Cru Bourgeois
Beautiful park and historical cellars. A pure Médoc.

These 'noses' represent 'the custodians of good wine'.

From Blanquefort, you could make a short detour to Le Taillan, just to the west, and visit the splendid Château du Taillan. In addition to its red Haut-Médoc, a white Bordeaux, Château La Dame Blanche, is produced here. White wines are rare in the Médoc, but more and more producers are planting white grapes besides black varieties.

Graves and Sauternes

South of Bordeaux there stretches a large winegrowing area that is divided into several very well-known appellations: Pessac-Léognan, Graves and Sauternes, to name just three of them. This is an area with a great diversity of wines. In the Graves district both red and white wines are produced; in Sauternes, the range is all white, with dry, semi-sweet or *moelleux* to chose from. The grape varieties blended to make them are Cabernet Sauvignon, Cabernet Franc and Merlot for the reds, and Sauvignon, Sémillon and Muscadelle for the whites.

Besides simple semi-sweet Graves Supérieurs and other basic wines, the area also produces reds and whites of high quality – of interest to every enthusiast. The Maison des Vins de Graves in Podensac offers valuable help in describing them: records and literature are good, there is a *vinothèque*, and the visitor is given a friendly and hospitable welcome, added to which the office is open all year round. There are about 100 châteaux in the area and apart from those in Pessac-Léognan, where it is customary to make an appointment, the estates are open practically every day to visitors. In many cases English is spoken.

The Graves district extends southeast past the town of Langon, interrupted by the vineyards of Cérons, Sauternes and Barsac, enclaves which have appellations of their own. The landscape in this part of the Bordeaux region is well worth exploring; the environs of La Brède, where Montesquieux's castle stands, are particularly beautiful. The Sauternes district, with its many châteaux, is just as picturesque. There are many spots in the Graves where you can enjoy a fine view of the wine districts on the opposite bank of the Garonne, too.

Left *The stunning, moated Château de Labrède, the birthplace and home of the famous statesman,* politician and writer, Montesquieu. The castle dates from the 13th century.

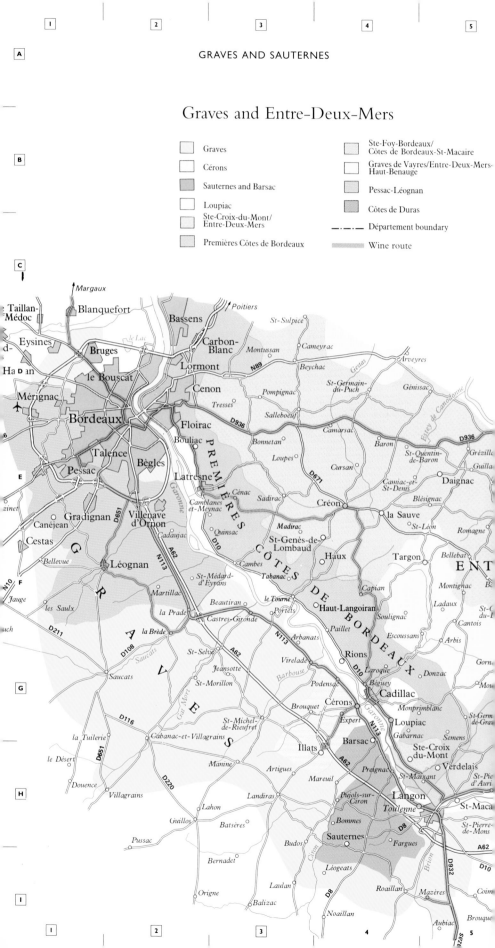

Graves

The southern suburbs

If you could transport yourself back in time to the Middle Ages you would see Bordeaux as a walled city, wholly centred on quayside activities along the River Garonne. Just to the south, the city was fringed by a semi-circle of parishes: Saint-Genès, Talence, Pessac and Bègles. These made up 'Graves de Bordeaux', the city's original winegrowing district. At this time, wine was already one of the region's major exports.

Today you must search amongst office blocks to find the vineyards, in so far as they still exist. Bègles is best known now for its rugby club, and Talence for its university – but redeems itself a little as home of the Institut d'Oenologie. The construction of the Mérignac airport also meant uprooting vines; a tiny vineyard near the perimeter has been kept as homage to the grape; for the rest it is all asphalt and concrete.

PESSAC-LEOGNAN

HOTELS

La Réserve
74 Avenue du Bourgailh (Alouette)
Tel: 56 07 13 28
A relief after the crowded city.
Luxurious rooms from around FF600,
swimming pool, tennis courts; good,
classic cuisine: set menus from FF160.

Royal Brion
10 Rue du Pin-Vert (Pessac)
Tel: 56 45 07 72
Comfortable rooms from about
FF300.

Hôtel Guyenne
Avenue François-Rabelais (Talence)
Tel: 56 80 75 08
Excellent hotel belonging to the locally
very well thought of *Lycée Hôtelier*.

RESTAURANTS

Les Chasseurs
Tel: 56 64 11 58 (Léognan)
Village restaurant, set lunch from FF85.

Grill La Forge
Tel: 56 64 11 58 (Léognan)
Good for a quick bite, from FF80.

Le Chalet Lyrique
Tel: 56 89 11 59 (Gradignan)
Pleasant hotel-restaurant. Spacious,
comfortable rooms from FF300. Meat
dishes prevail as the owner was once
a butcher. Set menus from FF200.

RECOMMENDED PRODUCERS

Château Bouscaut
Cru Classé *Tel: 56 30 72 40* (Cadaujac)
Splendid 18th-century estate. Since
1980, a Lurton property. Aromatic,
fresh white with a taste that lingers.

Château Picque-Caillou
Tel: 56 47 37 98 (Mérignac)
Smooth red; can drink young.

Château Haut-Brion
Grand Cru Classé (1er) (red)
Tel: 56 00 29 30 (Pessac) The only
Graves estate to be included in the 1855
classification. The large 16th-century
château used to be beyond the
Bordeaux town boundary, but is

PESSAC

Typical of post-World War II development is the
situation in Pessac, where such renowned
châteaux as Haut-Brion, La Mission Haut-Brion,
Les Carmes Haut-Brion and Pape Clément are
surrounded by flats and other dwellings. What
happened at Château Les Carmes Haut-Brion is
rather remarkable. The vineyard of this seven-
hectare estate is surrounded by a wall (which has
perhaps saved it from all the urban expansion). It
now appears, however, that the houses around this vineyard
provide it with extra protection, giving rise to a different,
warmer microclimate. The grapes at Château Les Carmes
Haut-Brion ripen earlier than anywhere else in Pessac.

Château Haut-Brion is the first name that springs to
mind when mentioning Pessac, and probably the first *grand
cru* to be exported out of the region. In 1664 Samuel Pepys,
the diarist and *bon vivant*, wrote that he had tasted 'Ho
Bryan, a wine of a new style and distinctive taste', at the
Royal Oak tavern in London's Lombard Street. Haut-Brion
had already been in existence for more than a century by
then. Its founder, Jean de Pontac, had begun in 1530 to buy
up plots around his '*maison noble*' and gradually pieced them
together into a vineyard. Château Haut-Brion was the only
Graves wine to be admitted into the *grands crus classés* in the
1855 classification.

On August 7th 1953 a first semi-official ranking of the
Graves *crus* was published. More important recognition
came on September 9th 1987, when the Pessac-Léognan
appellation contrôlée was granted. There are ten communities
in the suburbs and around the outskirts of Bordeaux that are
entitled to this: Cadaujac, Canéjan, Gradignan, Léognan,
Martillac, Mérignac, Pessac, Saint-Médard-d'Eyrans,
Talence, and Villenave d'Ornon. Of these communes,
Léognan, Martillac and Pessac are by far the most important.

LEOGNAN

The easiest way to get from Pessac to Léognan is via the ring road, leaving it at exit 18. Turn right immediately afterwards and then bear left when the road forks – this is the D651 which will take you right there. Léognan is one of the ten places that make up the Pessac-Léognan appellation and, with some 425 hectares of vineyards, it is its most important.

Léognan has about 20 of the 55 or so châteaux in Pessac-Léognan. Fifteen produce both red and white wines. One of the smallest estates in the whole of Bordeaux is to be found here: Domaine du Petit Bourdieu, with just 75 hectares and an average yield of 3,000 bottles of red wine a year.

The village itself does not perhaps amount to much, but it does have a Romanesque church (restored in the 19th century). Then in the centre there is a wine shop, the Caves de Léognan, next to the cellars of Château Malartic-Lagravière.

To start your tour of the Léognan and Martillac châteaux you should drive from the centre of the village up to the churchyard. Here the road to the left leads to Le Bouscat. By going right, then first left (onto the D109), you will come to Martillac. This route is highly recommended as it gives you a good view of the very gravelly soil (the *graves*), and the

now surrounded by suburbs. Noble, velvet-smooth red wine with sublime balance and long, gratifying aftertaste. Distinguished, long-lived white.

Château Les Carmes Haut-Brion
Tel: 56 51 49 43 (Pessac)
Deep-coloured, elegant red wine.

Château Pape Clément
Cru Classé *Tel: 56 07 04 11* (Pessac)
Established in 1300 by Archbishop Bertrand de Goth of Bordeaux, later Pope Clement V. Red wine with a broad, generous taste and strong constitution. White is less impressive.

Château La Mission Haut-Brion
Cru Classé *Tel: 56 00 29 30* (Talence)
Dark red wine of high quality.

Château Laville Haut-Brion
Cru Classé *Tel: 56 00 29 30* (Talence)
Outstanding white that needs years of maturing before reaching its best.

Château Latour Haut-Brion
Cru Classé *Tel: 56 00 29 30* (Talence)
Strong, complex red, rich in tannin.

Château Carbonnieux
Cru Classé *Tel: 56 87 08 28* (Léognan)
Famous old estate, taken over by Benedictine monks in 1741 – they exported their white wine to the (Muslim) Tukish court as 'mineral water'. Pale white wine with a clean, fresh taste. The red needs ageing.

Château de Fieuzal
Cru Classé *Tel: 56 64 77 86* (Léognan)
One of the district's best red wines. Plenty of fruit, tannin and a long finish. The white wine is just as good.

Château de France
Tel: 56 64 75 39 (Léognan)
Decent red wine with deep colour and a powerful aftertaste. The white is agreeable, supple and lightly fruity.

Château Haut-Bailly
Cru Classé *Tel: 56 64 75 11* (Léognan) An unspectacular-looking château making an almost satiny red wine of outstanding quality.

Château Larrivet Haut-Brion
Tel: 56 64 75 51 (Léognan)
Fragrant, fresh white wine. Structured red, needing some maturing.

Château Malartic-Lagravière
Cru Classé *Tel: 56 64 75 08* (Léognan)
Pleasing fresh white with a long, generous finish. The red, with deep colour and character, needs keeping.

Far left (top) *Immaculate vines belonging to Château Haut-Brion.* Far left (below) *Old steps at Château Olivier, a medieval moated fortress with a gravelly vineyard.* Left *Château Pape-Clément, a handsome property established in 1300.*

lie of the vineyards. A wine route, a *circuit touristique des crus classés*, has been set out, but the signposting in places leaves something to be desired. Two of the visually most attractive properties awaiting discovery here are Château La Louvière, built at the end of the 18th century by Victor Louis, the famous architect of Bordeaux's Grand Théâtre; and Château Olivier, a medieval stronghold with a moat around it. Nearly all the estates are open to visitors; in many cases, though, it is advisable to make an appointment beforehand. For a good meal many winegrowers prefer a restaurant in Gradignan.

MARTILLAC

When you drive from Léognan to Martillac (take the D109) you see before you a great expanse of wine district. After an action group – led by André Lurton – managed to stop valuable gravel soils being sacrificed to projects other than wine, the extension of the Martillac vineyards began. There is now

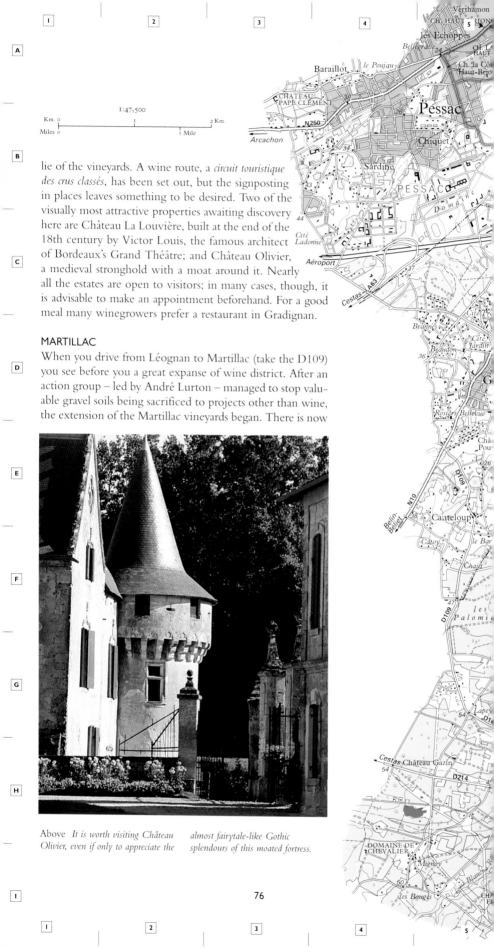

Above *It is worth visiting Château Olivier, even if only to appreciate the almost fairytale-like Gothic splendours of this moated fortress.*

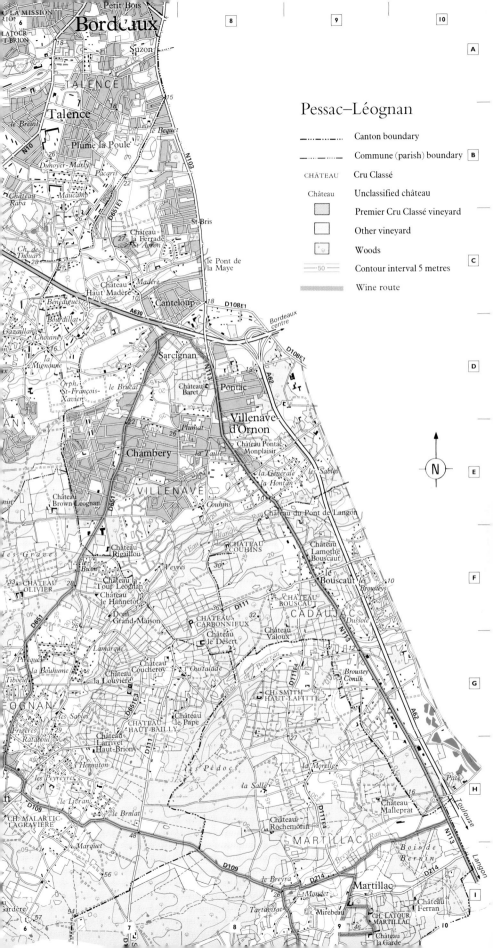

Pessac–Léognan

–·–··–·–·–	Canton boundary
–·–·–·–	Commune (parish) boundary
CHÂTEAU	Cru Classé
Château	Unclassified château
▨	Premier Cru Classé vineyard
▢	Other vineyard
⬚	Woods
—— 50 ——	Contour interval 5 metres
▨▨▨▨	Wine route

Château Olivier
Cru Classé *Tel: 56 64 73 31* (Léognan)
The château is a splendid medieval,
moated fortress. Gravelly vineyards
give fresh, clean white, elegant red.

Domaine de Chevalier
Cru Classé *Tel: 56 64 16 16* (Léognan)
This remarkable vineyard – in a
clearing deep in the woods behind
the village – makes magnificent white
wine that surpasses almost all other
dry white Bordeaux. It is made with
meticulous attention to detail. The
red is also excellent, tending to great
Médoc in personality: needing 10 to
20 years to show its true character.

MARTILLAC

 RESTAURANT

Hostellerie Lou Pistou
Tel: 56 23 71 02
Although it doesn't look as if it would
be from the outside, the cooking
here is good. Menus for under FF100.

 RECOMMENDED PRODUCERS

Château La Garde
Tel: 56 35 53 00 (Parempuyre)
Pleasant red wine, harmonious and
refined in its flavours. The same is
true of the white.

Château La Tour Martillac
Cru Classé *Tel: 56 72 71 21* (Martillac)
An unassuming château with an old
tower (the remains of a 12th-century
fort) in the inner courtyard. The red
wine has class. The white is a classic
dry Graves, improved with bottle age.

Château de Rochemorin
Tel: 57 25 58 58 (Grézillac)
Velvety, lasting red, with supple tannins.

*Above and far right Two aspects
of the charming town of Bazas, near
Langon: a Bazardaise cow and one
of the town's many beautiful streets.
Right Grapes in traditional leather
paniers at Château Pape-Clément.*

substantial investment into viticulture here, and it is safe to
assume that some wines of surprising quality will emerge.
Martillac has quite an elevated situation – rare in this region.

In the village there is a Romanesque church with some
interesting painted reliefs. A little way from the centre is the
Château La Tour Martillac, dating from 1750 and with a
tower even older in its courtyard. More or less facing it is
Château La Garde, with newly built cellars under the lawns.

LABREDE

Charles Louis de Segondat, Baron de la Brède et de
Montesquieu, was born at the castle of La Brède in 1689.
Thanks to this French philosopher, writer (*L'Esprit des lois*
and *Lettres persanes*), member of parliament
and mayor of Bordeaux, the name of the
village – and his own in the shortened form
Montesquieu – have remained well known.
The virtually unspoiled Gothic castle (dating
from the 13th and 15th centuries) has an
especially beautiful setting. It stands in a
moat and is surrounded by woods,
meadows and vineyards. There is said to be
an underground passage from the castle
to Château de Rochemorin, which also
belonged to Montesquieu. The castle is open

for visiting at weekends. His library there, with some 7,000 volumes, is still intact. The little village of Labrède, which borders on the Martillac district, has 100 hectares of vineyard, 80 percent of which is occupied by two producers.

PODENSAC AND ITS ENVIRONS

The A62 motorway divides the Graves area into two. The district south of Labrède, with its low-lying landscape of woods, meadows and maize fields, is of scant interest to the wine-lover. However, if you drive from Labrède on this motorway, or take the N113 *route nationale*, you will come to more interesting surroundings with wine villages such as Castres, Portets, and Podensac.

The most important sight to see in Portets is the Château de Portets, built in the 19th century on the foundations of a much older fortification. The château stands at the centre of a large park and has as its entrance an impressive wrought-iron gate (which appears on the wine labels). The village name derives from the word '*port*' – the harbour here used to handle considerable quantities of goods for export. Another sight worth exploring is the 18th-century Château de Mongeau, where there is a museum devoted to Waldec de Lessart, Louis XVI's last minister of foreign affairs.

Podensac has the excellent and helpful Maison du Vin de Graves. If you are travelling in the area you should really try

Château Smith Haut Lafitte
Cru Classé *Tel: 56 30 72 30* (Martillac)
Remarkable, fairly recent château and cellar complex amidst the vineyards. Both the white and red Pessac-Léognan wines seem to improve every vintage.

LABREDE

RESTAURANT

La Maison des Graves
Tel: 56 20 06 40
Restaurant in the centre of the village with fairly modern cuisine that includes *Saumon en Infusion de Graves*. Excellent list with many unfamiliar wines. Set menus from about FF100.

RECOMMENDED PRODUCERS

Château Magneau
Tel: 56 20 20 57
Full-bodied, refined white Graves that is soon ready for drinking. The red wine is firm, with fruit. The same family has owned this estate since the 17th century.
Château La Blancherie-Peyret
Tel: 56 20 20 39
Reserved wine with pleasant fragrance.

IN AND AROUND PODENSAC

RESTAURANTS

Le Bel Ombrage
Tel: 56 67 01 66 (Castres)
A simple restaurant with reasonable cooking. Set menus start around FF65.
Relais des Trois Mousquetaires
Tel: 56 27 09 07 (Podensac)
Relaxed restaurant with very good cooking. Classic regional dishes and a choice of three set menus all under FF100, each of them starting with soup.
Ma Vie La
Tel: 56 27 07 24 (Portets)
On the village square. Simple, but good and surprisingly inexpensive food (oysters, salads, *grillades* etc).

RECOMMENDED PRODUCERS

Château Ferrande
Tel: 56 67 05 86 (Castres)
The red wines are sound and stylish in bouquet and taste. Whites have a fruity smoothness.
Château de Chantegrive
Tel: 56 27 17 38 (Podensac)
Juicy red wine with distinct oaky notes. The white comes from older vines and has a complex bouquet and a good fresh taste.
Château de Mauves
Red wine of a high standard.

Château Cheret-Pitres
Tel: 56 67 27 76 (Portets)
Near the river (to get here take the road to Langoiran). Deep-coloured, meaty red Graves packed with juice and fruit.

Château du Grand Abord
Tel: 56 67 22 79 (Portets)
Full-flavoured, harmonious red wine, and fruity and very pure-tasting white.

Château Rahoul
Tel: 56 67 01 12 (Portets)
Outstanding white wine with a nuanced taste and a smooth, refined finish. The red, too, has style and distinction.

Château La Tour Bicheau
Tel: 56 67 37 75 (Portets)
A sturdy red, fruity Graves. The white is smooth with modest fruitiness.

Château La Vieille France
Tel: 56 67 19 11 (Portets)
Red wine with a smooth, supple, wood and tannin taste.

Domaine La Grave
Tel: 56 62 44 70 (Landiras)
Immaculate wines. The red is reliable: tannin-rich and with good body. The white has charming freshness.

Vieux Château Gaubert
Tel: 56 67 52 76 (Portets)
Tasting cellar and castle ruins. Very successful, almost masterly dry white wine, and refined, pure-tasting red.

Main picture *This pretty house is in the village of Portets, which produces some notable Graves wines.* Above *The local sweet vermouth, Lillet, is a surprisingly good and reasonably priced foil to foie gras.* Far right (top) *Château La Mission Haut-Brion.*

to visit it. There is also a well-stocked *vinothèque* where Pessac-Léognan wines are amongst those for sale.

Podensac also boasts its own aperitif based on wine, Lillet, and a related factory (in the main street) with an attractive museum that includes old posters and labels. Visitors are welcome and while there they can taste a glass of Lillet. Also worth spending time in is the Parc de Chavat where there is a remarkable sculpture collection.

CERONS

In the southern part of the Graves there are three districts with their own appellations. They are surrounded on all sides by the Graves and share its geological structure. These districts are Cérons, Barsac and Sauternes.

The small area around the village of Cérons is a transitional zone between Graves and Sauternes: here the four most important wines of the two areas, namely red, dry white, semi-sweet and sweet white are all made. This means in fact that various appellations are in use. The red and the dry white wines are sold as Graves, the semi-sweet whites as

Graves Supérieures, and the sweet as Cérons. (*Botrytis cinerea*, or 'noble rot', responsible for the lusciously sweet *vins liquoreux* occurs here, but a little less alluringly, perhaps, than further south in the famed appellations of Barsac and Sauternes.)

As early as the 3rd century AD there was mention of wines from '*Sirione*', and the name has ended up as Cérons. The old centre of this town lies between the N113 and the River Garonne. There is a 12th-century Romanesque church here, which has been later extended and enlarged. Opposite it stands Château de Cérons, built about three centuries ago by the Marquis de Calvimont. On the east side of the N113 is the village square, with an old market hall. The Syndicat Viticole – which in 1921 achieved the granting of the Cérons appellation – is here also.

Illats, also under Cérons jurisdiction, has an interesting 12th-century Romanesque church with a fine interior.

CERONS

HOTEL

La Grappe d'Or
Tel: 56 27 11 61
Simple hotel on the village square. Prices from around FF150. Has an unpretentious restaurant.

RECOMMENDED PRODUCERS

Château de Cérons
Tel: 56 27 01 13 (Cérons)
Sound, sweet white wine from a relatively small estate.

Château de Gravaillas
(Cérons) The best white wine here is the velvet-smooth 'Privilège'.

Château Lamouroux
Tel: 56 27 01 53 (Cérons)
A generous white Graves with a full, flavourful aftertaste.

Château d'Archambeau
Tel: 56 62 51 46 (Illats)
White wine with lovely pure fruit; supple-tasting, deep-coloured reds.

Château d'Ardennes
Tel: 56 62 53 80 (Illats)
Red wine with good depth of colour, and rich meatiness and juicy fruit on the palate. The white is creamy with an agreeable, fruity, rounded taste.

Château d'Arricaud
Tel: 56 62 51 29 (Landiras)
A semi-sweet Graves Supérieures with a good deal of breeding – which also applies to the dry white wine and the red.

Château Haut-Peyraguey
(Illats) Elegant red wine with a pleasing, rounded taste.

Château de Navarro
Tel: 56 27 20 27 (Illats)
White Graves Supérieures of a very good standard. The red wine has a somewhat fat, supple taste.

Château La Tuilerie
Tel: 56 62 53 80 (Illats)
Good, lively red and white wines, with distinctive personalities.

Sauternes and Barsac

The wines

About 25 kilometres south of Bordeaux there is a small district that produces one of the world's most amazing wines – Sauternes. Sauternes wines were included in the 1855 classification and were the only Bordeaux whites to be given this honour. But despite such an accolade, and although wine had been made there for hundreds of years, fame had not yet truly arrived. It was not until 1859 that the great international breakthrough began. In 1859 Russian Grand Duke Constantine visited Château d'Yquem and tasted a 12 year-old wine (1847 vintage). He was so impressed by it that he offered 20,000 gold francs for a *tonneau* (1,200 bottles). It was made from grapes picked later than usual, and which had rotted in a quite remarkable way. Château d'Yquem had therefore not put the wine on the market.

The secret of Sauternes lies in its micro-climate. In the autumn, cold water flows from the Ciron and other streams into the much warmer Garonne River, creating a morning mist that leaves a moist film on the grapes: the ideal growing medium for *Botrytis cinerea*, a tiny fungus that

Sauternes and Barsac

---·---·---	Canton boundary
---·---·---	Commune (parish) boundary
CHÂTEAU	Cru Classé
Château	Cru Bourgeois
▢	Premier Grand Cru Classé vineyard
▢	Other vineyard
▢	Woods
— 50 —	Contour interval 5 metres
	Wine route

1:41,500

Km. 0 _____ 1 _____ 2 Km

Miles 0 _____ 1 Mile

Below *Vines near the village of Pujols-sur-Ciron. Mists rising from the Ciron stream provides the perfect damp conditions for the development of* Botrytis cinerea *on warm, early autumn days.*

SAUTERNES AND BARSAC

HOTELS

Château de Valmont
Tel: 56 27 28 24 (Barsac)
Former wine estate, now 200 years
old. Above what was the cellar are 12
rooms all with excellent bathrooms.
Each room is named after a château,
a small bottle of whose wine
welcomes the guests. The rooms are
quiet, despite the popularity of this
hotel for weddings, etc. Prices from
about FF420. No restaurant but a
table d'hôte in season.

Château de Commarque
Tel: 56 76 65 94 (Sauternes)
Charming, small hotel with eight basic
rooms in a quiet situation. Prices from
below FF200. Pleasant, inexpensive
restaurant. English owners.

RESTAURANTS

**Hostellerie du Château du
Rolland**
Tel: 56 27 15 75 (Barsac)
Situated on the Ciron. Appetizing,
unpretentious dishes. Set menus from
about FF100. Also a few comfortable
rooms at prices starting around FF400.

La Table du Sauternais
Tel: 56 63 43 44 (Preignac)
An agreeable place to eat in the
centre of the Sauternes, with some
surprising and inventive dishes. Set
menus start below FF100.

Above *A sign advertises the
modest Maison de Sauternes.*
Top *Harvesting at Château
d'Yquem. No cost is spared here in
order to produce what is generally
regarded as the world's finest sweet
wine. The pickers are sent into the
vineyard as many times as necessary
to hand select only those botrytised
grapes that have reached peak
ripeness. This process can continue
for several weeks.*

causes a special form of rot in the grapes. Under the autumn
sun the mist has gone by about 11am, but by then the fungus will have settled on the grapes and started to affect them.

Unlike other kinds of rot, this one is exceedingly beneficial for the fruit. That is why it is called *pourriture noble*, or
'noble rot'. Through evaporation the affected grapes lose a
lot of their moisture, so that what is left is juice concentrated
into a syrup. A certain amount of acid is also lost and the
aroma of the grapes changes. The affected fruit does not
look very pleasant – it becomes rather shrivelled. But
appearances deceive, for this is the basis of golden Sauternes.

Pourriture noble can only occur on very ripe grapes. The
grower must wait until late on in the season before picking.
This is taking a great risk: the warm
autumn weather quite often breaks and
rain and cold lead to a wholly unsuccess-
ful crop. If, however, everything goes to
plan, the grapes are picked around the
end of October. This is done with the
very greatest care: bunches with over-ripe
grapes affected by the botrytis are selected
by hand. As the degree of ripeness can
vary even within the same vineyard, the
pickers need to search the vines several
times over. Weeks are needed to carry
out what normally takes only few days.

The harvesting alone makes Sauternes much more
expensive than other wines. The yields are low, too. A vinicultural rule of thumb is that every vine produces one bottle
of wine. At Château d'Yquem every vine gives just one
glass! The legally permitted maximum yield is 25 hectolitres
of wine per hectare; many do not even reach this low figure.

A good Sauternes is a complex wine with surprising
effects on all the senses. A beautiful, intense golden colour
is followed by a richly nuanced bouquet with impressions of
honey, nuts and apricots. The taste is improved by age: some

84

young Sauternes, however fresh and pure, have much less depth and complexity than those with some maturity.

Sauternes from recent vintages are often drunk as aperitifs, or with *pâté de foie gras* (a somewhat lighter Loupiac is often preferred with duck's liver). Older, mature Sauternes can go excellently with the blue-veined Roquefort cheeses.

The region

The Sauternes district is divided into five communes: Barsac, Preignac, Bommes, Fargues, and Sauternes. The most northern is Barsac. This is distinct from all the others in that it is entitled to its own appellation, 'Barsac', as well as AC Sauternes. The Barsac landscape is fairly flat, Preignac's less so, while in Bommes, Fargues and Sauternes there are some decent hills.

Barsac is the oldest wine village hereabouts: the remains of Roman villas have been found beside the church. By the main door of this church there are two marks showing how high the River Garonne reached in the floods of 1770 and 1930.

Preignac is a typical main road village, with an 18th-century church (with a cupola), and a few wine-tasting rooms.

Le Saprien
Tel: 56 63 60 87 (Sauternes)
The area's best restaurant outside Langon, with a pleasant garden and terrace. Recommended is the *soupe de crustacés parfumée au safran*. Set menus from about FF120 (cheaper lunch menu).

Auberge les Vignes
Tel: 56 76 60 06 (Sauternes)
Convivial restaurant by the Place de l'Eglise, serving classic regional dishes. Set menus from about FF75.

RECOMMENDED PRODUCERS

Château Broustet
Cru Classé (2ème)
Tel: 57 24 70 79 (Barsac)
Balanced, sound Barsac with a reserved luxuriousness about it, a flawless perfume and a long finish.

Château Climens
Cru Classé (1er)
Tel: 56 27 15 33 (Barsac)
Refined, rich, elegant wine.

Château Coutet
Cru Classé (1er)
Tel: 56 27 15 46 (Barsac)
Noble, refined Barsac. In really great years a 'Cuvée Madame' is made. A lovely dry Graves is also produced.

Château Gravas
Tel: 56 27 15 20 (Barsac)
Wine with a golden lustre and a delicous touch of *pourriture noble*.

Château Nairac
Cru Classé (2ème)
Tel: 56 27 16 16 (Barsac)
Sauternes with style and finesse.

Château La Tour-Blanche
Cru Classé (1er)
Tel: 56 76 61 55 (Bommes)
Remarkable wine from the agricultural school here: it has a fresh aroma and a delicious concentrated taste.

Château de Fargues
Tel: 56 63 21 05 (Fargues)
Same owner as d'Yquem. The wine is made with the same perfection, it is a little less bounteous, but still very fine.

Château Lafaurie-Peyraguey
Cru Classé ((1er)
Tel: 56 31 44 44 (Fargues)
Wine with style and an intense richness of bouquet and taste.

Château Rieussec
Cru Classé (1er)
Tel: 42 56 33 50 (Fargues)
Impressive sweet wine; among best in the area. Fine palate and concentrated finish. Also notable dry white.

Left *Château Bastor-Lamontagne in the commune of Preignac produces remarkable Sauternes, belying its cru bourgeois status.*

Château Bastor Lamontagne
Tel: 56 63 27 66 (Preignac)
Great, luxurious; rival to *crus classés*.

Château Gillette
(Preignac) Remarkable wine that
matures for at least 20 years before
being bottled. Very vital, with a sweet
taste of caramel and honey.

Château Haut-Bergeron
Tel: 56 63 24 76 (Preignac) Golden,
generous Sauternes, with many awards.

Château de Malle
Cru Classé (2ème)
Tel: 56 63 28 67 (Preignac)
In good years this is a complex,
intense wine. A good red wine –
Château de Cardaillan – is also made.

Château Suduiraut
Cru Classé (1er)
Tel: 56 63 27 29 (Preignac)
An almost decadently luxurious wine.

Château d'Arche
Cru Classé (2ème)
Tel: 56 76 66 55 (Sauternes)
Luxurious, aromatic; long aftertaste.

Château Guiraud
Cru Classé (1er)
Tel: 56 76 61 01 (Sauternes)
Strikingly fresh, complex Sauternes.

Château Raymond-Lafon
(Sauternes) Made in the same way as
d'Yquem – a luxurious sweet wine.

Château d'Yquem
Premier Cru Supérieur
Tel: 56 63 21 05 (Sauternes)
Legendary, very expensive wine, the
very best Sauternes and a feast for
the senses, as is dry wine 'Y'.

Main picture *Harvesting at
Château d'Arche, one of the three
properties in Sauternes classified in
1855 as a second growth.*
Below *The Maison du Vin, in the
Place de la Mairie in Sauternes, sells
a variety of local wines.*

Signposts show the way to Château de Malle, a historic
monument well worth a visit. Flanked by its pepper-pot
towers, this 17th-century building has Italian gardens and a
large collection of *objets d'art* and furniture, as well as some
interesting fireplaces, a fine chapel and the most important
collection of silhouettes in Europe. These are lifesize figures
carved in wood. They were used both in theatrical perfor-
mances and as firescreens when hearths blazed too fiercely.

Bommes is a small village, settled around a Romanesque
church. Worht a visit is Château Lafaurie-Peyraguey, a castle dating in part from the 13th century.

Sauternes is especially pretty if
you drive there from Bommes,
approaching from a slope leading
down into the village. On the
wide, bare square, the Maison du
Vin stocks well-known châteaux
wines and a good own-brand wine.
The most impressive château in
every respect here is d'Yquem,
resplendent in its unapproachable-
ness on its 75-metre hill.

With its gently sloping hills, the
Sauternes district is a very pleasant
area to visit. There is a well-
signposted *Circuit du Sauternais* to

explore, too – the châteaux are easy to find if you follow the signs. Driving round does not take long: it is a small area. The Ciron Valley is particularly appealing. It is best simply to leave the car and walk; it is an ideal setting for a picnic.

Langon and its environs

Langon is where the people of the Sauternes do their weekly shopping, and there is a busy Saturday market. The town is at a meeting of the ways: Les Landes, Entre-Deux-Mers and the motorway to Toulouse are within easy reach. The quays along the River Garonne are lovely to walk along.

About 10 kilometres to the south, between Langon and Bazas, is Mazères with its Château de Roquetaillade. This is a massive, 14th-century castle. Near to it are the ruins of a more primitive fortification, the Saint-Michel chapel with its oriental interior, and a 13th-century dovecot.

And rather more interesting than Langon is the old fortified town of Bazas. There is another bustling market here, held on the square in front of the Gothic cathedral. Cattle are chased through the streets on the Thursday before Shrovetide – the town has given its name to good quality beef, *boeuf de Bazas*. In this pleasant little town there is a unique and not very well known museum of antiquities with an *apothicairerie*, or apothecary's shop. The Saint-Antoine hospital used to be outside the town gates and was intended for the care of pilgrims going to Santiago de Compostela.

LANGON

RESTAURANTS

Les Remparts
Tel: 56 25 95 24 (Bazas)
On the walls of this attractive little town there is an excellent place to eat: Les Remparts serves classic cuisine with, eg, *chapon grignolais aux cèpes*. Set menus from about FF80.

Claude Darroze
Tel: 56 63 00 48 (Bazas)
Darroze belongs amongst the very greatest in the Gironde. A summertime meal on the terrace here is a unique experience. The modern cuisine has a classic basis. Customers are made to feel very welcome. Set menus from about FF300. Nicely furnished rooms at around FF350.

Le Brion
Tel: 56 76 27 75
Pleasant restaurant where the décor creates the atmosphere. Modern interpretations of regional fare. Set menus from about FF100.

RECOMMENDED PRODUCERS

Château Brondelle
Tel: 56 62 38 14 (Langon)
Respectable, not over-firm red Graves; cool-tasting, fragrant and fruity white.

Château Camus
Tel: 56 63 19 34 (St-Pierre de Mons)
Honest red Graves, agreeably fruity.

Château Chicane
Rounded red wine with plenty of colour, and fruit on the palate.

Château de Courbon
Pleasing, complete white Graves with fruitiness and a smooth, fresh taste.

Clos Floridène
The white is fresh and robust, with a slight hint of wood. The red has a pleasant raspberry and bilberry aromas, and a rounded, firm palate.

Château Montalivet
Smooth, fresh white wine with a distinguished aroma of wood with vanilla. The red is well structured with a very pleasant suppleness and flavour.

Château Respide Médeville
Tel: 56 63 27 59 (Preignac)
Both the red and white are among the better Graves wines: the white is luxurious and full of character, the red is distinguished by its fruit and wood.

Château St-Robert
Tel: 56 63 27 66 (Preignac)
Outstanding red Graves; newish estate.

Domaine de Gaillat
Tel: 56 63 50 52 (Langon)
Deep dark notes of leather, and dried prune flavours supported by good tannin, give this wine great breeding.

Entre-Deux-Mers

The *mers* ('seas') are in fact two tidal rivers – the Dordogne and the Garonne – the ebb and flow of which are perceptible even above Libourne. These form the two natural boundaries of Entre-Deux-Mers. The third boundary containing this wedge-shaped district is the eastern border of the Gironde *département*. Entre-Deux-Mers is the largest Bordeaux wine area, stretching for 80 kilometres southeast of the town, 30 kilometres across at its widest point.

This land of two rivers is made up of various appellations, of which Entre-Deux-Mers itself is by far the most important. Until the 1970s its semi-sweet, somewhat insipid wines were of barely any interest to wine-lovers. But quality has made great strides forward and today the name is used exclusively for sound dry whites. In terms of the wines you encounter, however, there is everything here, from strong reds and light rosés, to dry and fully sweet whites.

Entre-Deux-Mers reds remain of key importance: many Bordeaux brand names owe their existence to them. The hilly appellation of Premières Côtes de Bordeaux in the west is a nursery for an increasing number. Also well worth discovering are the sweet wines of Cadillac. And further south along the Garonne, there are two enclaves, Loupiac and Sainte-Croix-du-Mont. These lie directly opposite Sauternes and produce comparable dessert white wines, if perhaps rather less rich, sweet or intense. Further south again comes the Bordeaux-Saint-Macaire appellation; most of its red wine is sold as Bordeaux or Bordeaux Supérieur, although now and then you will come across a white. In the extreme northeast there is the Sainte-Foy-Bordeaux area, and in the northwest, between Libourne and Bordeaux, the relatively unknown Graves de Vayres for pleasant red and dry white wines.

Left *Oyster-catching and farming is widespread in the Entre-Deux-Mers region. The oysters are delicious* served with the crisp dry white wines *of the area, particularly those based on Sauvignon Blanc.*

Right *Château de Tastes'
remarkable wine is made entirely
from grapes from a single hectare of
Sauvignon Blanc vines in Ste-Croix
du Mont. It is owned by Bruno
Prats (also the owner of Cos
d'Estournel) and dates from 1230.*

ENTRE-DEUX-MERS

 HOTELS

Château de la Tour
Tel: 56 76 92 00 (Beguey)
With a view over the nearby castle at
Cadillac. Comfortable rooms from
about FF475. Swimming pool, terrace,
and restaurant serving classic dishes
(menus from about FF135).

Le Saint-Martin
Tel: 56 67 02 67 (Langoiran)
On the river, and therefore fairly
quiet. Small, pleasant rooms in light
colours; miniscule bathrooms. Prices
start under FF300. Cosy restaurant
with set menus from about FF100.
Also ideal as a base for visiting the
Graves region, only minutes away
across the bridge.

Château Lardier
Tel: 57 40 54 11 (Ruch)
Peaceful hotel surrounded by
vineyards. About 15 minutes from
Castillon-la-Bataille. Its nine rooms are
well kept (prices about FF300). In the
restaurant, set menus start at about
FF135. Also a wine estate.

Château de Malromé
Tel: 56 63 74 92 (St-André-du-Bois)
Very comfortable *chambres d'hôte* in
the château where Toulouse-Lautrec
passed his final years. Prices between
about FF350 and FF650.

Grand Hôtel
Tel: 57 46 00 08 (Ste-Foy-la-Grande)
In the main street (parking nearby).
Decent rooms with high ceilings
(prices from about FF300). On warm
days, lunch and dinner are served on
the terrace. Good regional food in
generous helpings (from about FF135
for a set menu). An excellent starting
point for the discovery of the
charming Ste-Foy Bordeaux district.

 RESTAURANTS

St-James (Bouliac)
For years now this has been the best
place to eat in the Gironde. Worth a
detour for the excellent, inventive
cooking of Jean-Marie Amat. Set menus
from around FF300. Long, impressive
wine list. St-James also owns the
Hauterive-Hôtel. The rooms here are
not just contemporary but positively
progressive. Prices from FF650.

Between the rivers
Entre-Deux-Mers, between the Dordogne and Garonne
rivers, is an extensive area with many monasteries, abbeys,
Romanesque churches, forts, castles and small fortified
towns, or *bastides* – all are reminders of the wars between the
French and English, which came to an end in 1453. The
landscape is one of hills and valleys, offering ever-changing
views out over vineyards, meadows, woods and fields.

Routes
From Bordeaux there are a number of possible sight-seeing
routes. The choice will depend on your interests and time
available. As a guideline, a complete circular tour will take
at least a day. One possible route is Bordeaux, Floirac,
Latresne, Créon, Cadillac, La Réole, Monségur, Sauveterre-
de-Guyenne, Castelviel, Rauzan, Branne, then Bordeaux.

In Quinsac at the Maison du Vin for the Premières Côtes
de Bordeaux there is a detailed route map available (*Balades*

Le Bistroy
Tel: 56 20 52 19 (Bouliac)
A simpler edition of the St-James, but with equally tasty cooking. Set menus start below FF200. To be avoided on hot, sunny days as the tables are set in the conservatory.

Hôtel de France
Tel: 56 84 50 06 (Branne)
On the market square, and a good place to eat. Classic cuisine with regional dishes such as *sole aux cèpes* and *profiterols au chocolat*. Set menus from around FF100. Rooms about FF250.

La Maison du Fleuve
Tel: 56 20 06 40 (Camblanes)
Louisiana-style restaurant built out on piles in the Garonne: a whole new concept for French gastronomy. Agreeable new-style cuisine such as *vol-au-vent d'escargots à la Bordelaise*. Set menus start at about FF100.

Marc Demund
Tel: 56 74 72 28 (Carbon Blanc)
Excellent restaurant in an unexpected setting, close to the A10 motorway. Inventive cooking: some outstanding dishes. Set menus from FF180.

Château Camiac
Tel: 56 23 20 85 (Créon)
This romantic 19th-century château is on the road to Branne. Classic cuisine with some new influences, as in *poêlée de ris de veau et de langoustines*. Set menus from about FF200.

La Fontine
Tel: 56 61 11 81 (Fontet)
Popular restaurant serving regional dishes, such as *magret grillé escaloppé de foie gras*. Set menus from FF60.

Les Remparts
Tel: 56 47 43 46 (Gensac)
Here, with a lovely view of the valley, you can enjoy the food in one of the up-and-coming restaurants of the Ste-Foy Bordeaux region. Set menus from about FF100.

Les Trois Cèdres
Tel: 56 71 10 70 (Gironde-sur-Dropt)
From the outside you would not think there was a young master-chef in the kitchen. Surprising cuisine – for example, *blignis de guanaja et caviar de pommes au nougat*. Set menus start around FF120. There are a few rooms here at about FF300 (always ask for one at the back).

La Belvédere
Tel: 57 47 40 33 (Juillac)
Perched on a high hill near the Dordogne. Apart from the splendid view, you can enjoy regional specialities here, like *magret* and *confit de canard*. Set menus from about FF100. Follow the signs from the village.

en Premières Côtes de Bordeaux) for this particular appellation. And the modern Maison de Qualité at Beychac-et-Cailleau, set up on the combined initiative of the Bordeaux producers, serves as an information centre for visits to wine estates. There is also a well-stocked *vinothèque* in the basement.

Useful route descriptions are also available at the Office du Tourisme in Bordeaux. These relate to themes other than wine: *circuit des églises fortifiées, circuit des villes fortifiées, circuit des souterrains* and of course *les bastides de la Gironde*. All the routes cover distances of 140 to 200 kilometres. What follows below are the sights to see, the restaurants, and the wine producers in the most important of the small towns and villages of the area. To help the reader they have been put in alphabetical order.

Baurech dates back to the Verego Roman villa, residence of Leontius II and a large wine estate of the time. In **Béguey** a splendid panorama of the surrounding country can be seen from the highest point in the hills. Architectural high points

Le Coq Sauvage
Tel: 56 20 41 04 (St-Loubes)
By the little harbour on the
Dordogne stands this congenial
restaurant, with an attractive indoor
garden. Classic, appetizing regional
dishes; set menus from about FF120.
Six rooms available, around FF300.

Au Vieux Logis
Tel: 56 78 92 99 (St-Loubes)
This well-known restaurant with its
good cooking is five minutes from the
golf course. Set menus start at
around FF120. Within 150m there is
a small hotel with simple, clean
rooms (ask for one at the back).
Prices from about FF250.

L'Abricotier
Tel: 56 76 83 63 (St-Macaire)
The décor in this restaurant is
contemporary, as is the chef's
culinary skill: *fondant de courgettes à la
menthe*, for example, or *mousse de
fromage blanc au miel*. Ample set
menus, from about FF100.

RECOMMENDED PRODUCERS

Château de Beau Rivage
Laguens (Baurech)
Well-structured wine with depth of
colour and hints of wood and fruit.

Château Melin
Tel: 56 21 34 71 (Baurech)
Dry white wine with a balanced taste,
and fruit character.

Château Reynon
Tel: 56 62 96 51 (Béguey)
Outstanding dry white wine, with
subtle aromas, and elegant yet juicy
fruit. The red (a Premières Côtes de
Bordeaux) is deep-coloured, powerful,
with fruit, vanilla and good length.

Château Lesparre
(Beychac-et-Cailleau)
Elegant, balanced red wine, with
vitality and deep colour.

Château Glaudet (Blasimon)
Wine from the Vignerons de
Guyenne. Fruity red wine.

Château les Gauthiers
(Bonnetan)
This small vineyard delivers a
scintillating red wine, meaty and with
concentrated fruit on the nose and
palate.

Château Fort-Bayard
(Branne)
Big red wine with plenty of tannin,
but with a supple and mouth-filling
taste none the less. The white wine,
too, merits a mention for its fruit
and charm.

Château David La Closière
(Cadillac)
Fresh white wine with a lot of fruit; at
its best when young.

are the remains of a Roman harbour wall and the 18th-
century Peyran estate. In **Beychac-et-Cailleau** there are two
attractions: an excellent golf course and the Maison de Qualité
– an embassy figure for Bordeaux producers.

Blasimon's Benedictine abbey (largely in ruins) has a
marvellous main door with allegorical representations of the
virtues and vices surrounding it. A small collection of archaeological finds is displayed in the *mairie*. **Bouliac**, is set quite
high up, and is best known for its restaurants. It has a 12th-
century church well worth seeing, too, built on the foundations of the Roman villa Vodol (Vodollacum Bodollacum
became Bouliac), and a noted place of refuge during the
Hundred Years War. **Branne** is a small harbour on the
Dordogne near Libourne, at its most beautiful in the light of
the setting sun. Its neo-Gothic church is 19th-century.

Cadillac has its own appellation – for sweet whites (Cadillac
red wine is sold as Bordeaux or Bordeaux Supérieur). The
town itself, founded in the 13th century, is still partly walled.
In the centre there stands an imposing castle of the ducs
d'Epernon – now home to the Maison du Vin. This stronghold was built in the 17th century, and its past functions
have included a spell as a women's prison. Inside are rooms
with great fireplaces and beautifully painted ceilings. An
important market is held in the town every Saturday.

In **Cambes** the interior of the Romanesque church of
Saint-Martin has been classified as a historic monument.
Also worth seeing here is the Château du Peyrat, built in
1655. And at **Camblanes et Meynac** around the church there

is a pleasant terrace, and a Roman mosaic in the *mairie*. **Capian** is well worth a visit to see its old mill foundations (many excavations have been carried out), the medieval tower used by the Télégraphe de Chappe, and the Romanesque church of Saint-Saturnin, where a Roman wine cask is preserved. Attractive sight-seeing routes are set out.

Carignan de Bordeaux for centuries now has been an area where well-to-do Bordeaux citizens have relaxed in environs steeped in history. The castles of Carignan (parts of it 15th century) and Canteloup (also a well-known wine estate), make fascinating visits, as does the 12th-century church. Then in **Castelviel** the local church, sited on a hill, has a beautiful porch; one of the reliefs shows a vine being pruned.

Cénac, an important stopping place for pilgrims en route to Santiago de Compostela, lies in particularly beautiful surroundings, with much to explore. A splendid view across the River Garonne can be enjoyed between Cénac and Montillac. And near **Créon** stands the most famous abbey of

Château Fayau
Tel: 56 62 65 80 (Cadillac)
Good red Bordeaux Supérieur with intense aroma and long length. The sweet white is sound and has often won awards.

Clos des Capucins (Cadillac)
Elegant white Bordeaux, dominated by the Sauvignon grape.

Château Melin (Cambes)
Reliable, attractive red wine. The rosé and the (fairly) sweet wines also merit attention.

Left *The Château de Cadillac, a 12th-century fortress, which produces red and white Bordeaux and Bordeaux Supérieur.*
Below *The Premières Côtes de Bordeaux. Some semi-sweet white wines are made, but the Merlot-based reds deserve most attention.*

93

Above The dramatic remains of a 13th-century fortress and keep at Langoiran, in the southern part of the Premières Côtes de Bordeaux.

Château Brethous
Tel: 56 20 77 76
(Camblanes-et-Meynac)
One of the oldest winegrowers in Camblanes. In good years produces a firm, supple red wine.

Château du Grand Moueys
Tel: 56 72 31 01 (Capian)
Lively, fresh and elegant red wine.

Château Rauzé-Lafargue
(Cénac) Wine from a relatively new vineyard, with a decent amount of fruit in its taste.

Domaine de la Meulière
(Cénac) Carefully made red wine, fragrant, balanced and complete.

Château Bauduc
Tel: 56 23 23 58 (Créon)
The *cuvée* Les Trois Hectares is an attractive white wine with a delicate, flowery aroma and a harmonious aftertaste, supported by a slight hint of wood.

Entre-Deux-Mers, La Sauve Majeure. Its tower dates from 1230 and is still in good, climbable condition: the view from the top is most impressive. The abbey itself (dating from 1079) is rather dilapidated but fascinating. There is also a museum.

Espiet exemplifies the fact that besides the *bastides* and fortified churches in Entre-Deux-Mers there are also fortified mills: Moulin Neuf here is one of the most elegant. So is the fountain of Saint-Aignan: its water was said to cure eye troubles and leprosy. **Gabarnac**'s 12th-century Romanesque church is a gem – especially for its main door, a classified historic monument. There are also two old 18th-century mills in the village. A visit to the mill in **Gornac** is also recommended (by appointment). Inside is a country life museum.

Haux is a 16th-century château, rebuilt as a fortress in the 17th century, surviving now as a wine estate. Wines from past vintages can be bought here. In **Langoiran** the Château de Langoiran is now little more than a ruin, but in the old stone quarries (*carrières*) excellent wines are matured. There is also a 12th-century church, a botanical park (the Parc de Peyruche) and a zoo. **Lestiac**, close to Château de Langoiran, is a traditional fishing spot, and a notable location for catching *aloses* (shad). And **Loubes** has one of the finest fortified mills in Entre-Deux-Mers, with entrance ways on two storeys. (It was built this way to cope when the floods came.)

Loupiac has a growing reputation in France. Its wines are white, full-flavoured and almost liqueur-like – very like Sainte-Croix-du-Mont. Locally they are drunk young as aperitifs, and taste excellent with *foie de canard*. Older wines deliciously complement fruit tarts. An archaeological dig in Loupiac has exposed a Roman bath complete with mosaics. Its church has been declared a monument and is also worth a visit.

The charming village of **Quinsac** houses the Maison du Vin for the Premières Côtes de Bordeaux. It has an engaging fountain let into the wall of the presbytery, the *fontaine du Clairet*. There is a market on Wednesdays. Then, above the village of **Rauzan**, are the ruins of Château de Duras (12–15th century). One of the largest and best of the French cooperatives is here, too, the Union de Producteurs de Rauzan.

Close to the little town of **La Réole** the abbey of Saint-Ferme still survives. It was built by Cluniac monks and partly rebuilt after 1585 – today it serves as a town hall. The monumental fireplace in its west wing is particularly striking. Thursday is La Réole's market day. Medieval **Rions** is known as 'Carcassonne of the Gironde', and there is some similarity to the famous fortified town. Its surrounding 14th-century walls are not the only architectural high points: others are the Tour du Lhyan, the citadel, the Charles VII cave, and the 12th-century church. **Saint-André-du-Bois**'s church has little history to recount, but the impressive cedars that stand around it could tell some tales. The village is most famous as home to artist Toulouse-Lautrec, who lived in the Château de Malromé – reproductions of his paintings hang in the château. A few *chambres d'hôte* are available. Then, well worth seeing at **Saint-Caprais de Bordeaux**, is the 11th- and 12th-century church. A Virgin and Child here are among some of the top examples of French medieval sculpture.

Sainte-Croix-du-Mont is well known for its sweet white wines, sometimes reaching the richness of Sauternes. The

Château Roques Mauriac (Doulezon) The Hélène *cuvée* is one of the great stars in Entre-Deux-Mers. This red wine is matured in wood and is packed with fruit. There is also a rather more run-of-the-mill red wine kept in steel tanks, but it also rates a recommendation.

Château Bonnet (Grézillac) Juicy, mouth-filling white wine with appealing aromas of fruit and spring flowers. The fruity, supple red wine is also pleasing.

Château de Haux (Haux) Outstanding white *première cuvée* with a rich, complex character.

Château Lamothe de Haux Tel: 56 23 05 07 (Haux) Dry white wine with a complex bouquet and a rich, full taste.

Château de Langoiran Tel: 56 67 08 55 (Langoiran) Excellent red wine matured in oak.

Château Tanesse Tel: 56 31 44 44 (Langoiran) Decent, soundly made red wine, with a discreet touch of oak.

Château de Seguin (Lignan) A Bordeaux Supérieur that regularly wins medals. Harmonious wine, supple and strong in its finish. Deserves a few years' patience.

Château du Vieux Moulin (Loupiac) One of the most beautiful small châteaux hereabouts, producing a luscious, carefully made wine.

Clos Jean (Loupiac) Dry white – from a village known for its sweet wine. A rich aroma and a deep, complex taste characterize this wine. The red rates good value.

Château Roquefort (Lugasson) White wine (Cuvée Spéciale) matured in wood, with a flowery, complex aftertaste.

Domaine de Chastelet Tel: 56 20 86 20 or 56 72 61 96 (Quinsac) Deep-coloured wine with dominant oak on the nose and the palate.

Château Vincy (Rauzan) Merlot is dominant in this deeply coloured wine, packed with ripe red fruit and with a long length.

Comte de Rudel (Rauzan) Red brand wine from the cooperative. Fruity with a juicy finish.

Left Loupiac produces sweet white wines that are rich and liqueur-like and, along with those of Ste-Croix-du-Mont, offer good value alternatives to Sauternes and Barsac.

locals drink them as aperitifs, and with poultry, white meat and game. There is a tasting cellar in one of the local *caves* where you can sample them. From the church square there is a splendid view out over the valley of the Garonne, Sauternes and the Graves district. The village is also renowned for its fossil oyster beds and Château de Tastes, a castle dating from the 14th and 15th centuries.

Sainte-Foy-la-Grande is a little hamlet steeped in history. As you walk through there are a number of ancient buildings and crumbling old fortifications. And in **Saint-Germain-du-Puch**, a simple wine village hiding more clues to the past than you'd expect, there are Roman mosaics in the church and a model of 14th-century military architecture in the Château du Grand Puch.

Medieval **Saint-Macaire**, built on a cliff, gives its name to the Côtes de Bordeaux Saint-Macaire appellation. Good to see are the merchants' houses, the intricate arcading on the square, the defensive walls, and the church. Also there is the Aquitaine postal museum and a museum of tropical fish.

R Rauzan Réserve (Rauzan)
Dry, white brand wine with a distinctive aroma and rich palate.
Château de Rions (Rions)
Smooth, fruity white wine.
Château Loubans
(Ste-Croix-du-Mont) Distinguished, luscious, almost creamy wine.
Château Lousteau-Vieil
(Ste-Croix-du-Mont) Wonderful sweet wine that can be compared to a Barsac.
Château La Rame
(Ste-Croix-du-Mont) Unctuous wine for keeping.
Château Jonqueyres
(St-Germain-du-Puch) Intense red wine with smooth, supple tannin and packed with fruit.
Château de Malagar
Tel: 56 31 44 44 (St-Maixant)
Elegant, attractive red wine and two decent white ones.
Château Le Grand Verdus
(Sadirac)
Splendid, perfectly structured red wine with delicious hints of oak.
Château de Beaulieu
(Sauveterre-de-Guyenne)
Red wine from the cooperative. Robust, fruity structure and a long aftertaste.
Domaine du Bourdieu (Soulignac)
Versatile estate that for some 20 years has been employing agrobiological methods of winegrowing. Good results in red, white and rosé.

The French author François Mauriac often spent time at Château de Malagar in **Saint-Maixant**. Mauriac was involved in trying out the various pathways (on horseback, bicycle or foot) now marked around the village. The château functions as a museum and a wine estate. **Sauveterre-de-Guyenne** is an attractive *bastide* with four of its original gateways. At the Bassellerie bakery here you can buy excellent *pain à l'ancienne* – traditional bread. Then in **Soulignac** the focal point is a windmill – the only one in Entre-Deux-Mers built to produce electricity. The village of **Targon** is best known for its Romanesque-style church. And the great attraction of **Vayres** is the castle, once the property of Henry IV of France, and now used as a conference centre. It has a fine terrace with a very large flight of steps and a garden that leads down to the Gironde. Also impressive is the *pigeonnier*, potentially home to some 2,600 birds. Vayres is the centre of the small wine district of Graves de Vayre, making supple red and white wines. The latter used to be semi-sweet, but fortunately are now following the trend towards dry wines.

Finally **Verdelais**, which has a notable basilica, built over eight centuries: Romanesque, Gothic and Baroque in style. Henri de Toulouse-Lautrec lies buried in the cemetery here.

Far left and main picture *The monumental Château de Vayres which attracts many visitors.*
Above *Spraying protects vines from insects and fungal diseases.*

Château la Clyde
Tel: 56 67 56 84 or 56 37 41 78 (Tabanac)
One of the best red wines from the Premières Côtes de Bordeaux: generous, firm and supple.

Château de Plassac
Tel: 56 67 53 16 (Tabanac)
At the end of the Revolution, the Clauzel family rebuilt the château in a Palladian style. The ordinary white wine here has a good taste.
The *cuvée spéciale* is rich, with a hint of wood.

Château Toutigeac
Tel: 56 23 90 10 (Targon)
For his white wine (100% Sémillon) the owner uses the Entre-Deux-Mers Haut Benauge appellation. This juicy wine, with minerally tones, ressembles white Graves. The red wine is well-balanced.

Château Bussac (Vayres)
Generous, mouth-filling white wine.

SPECIAL INTEREST

An artist works in the hamlet of Morizès, near to La Réole (telephone 56 71 45 56); her speciality is handmade roof tiles fired in a Gallo-Roman oven.

On 25th November the fountain at Camblanes-et-Meynac spouts free wine, as does the one at Quinsac.

In Vayres, a craftsman cooper – a tonnelier – is still at work; he can be visited by appointment (telephone 56 74 85 29).

The Libournais

On the right bank of the Dordogne lie two of the most renowned wine districts on earth: Saint-Emilion and Pomerol. Strangely enough, however, it was well into the 20th century before wines from these areas had any reputation at all; in France they were known, but few people abroad had ever heard of them. When the classification of the best Bordeaux wines was drawn up in 1855, the products of this area, the Libournais (centred on the town of Libourne), were not even considered – a fact scarcely imaginable today.

The Saint-Emilion district is bounded at the north by the little River Barbanne, to the east by the hills around Castillon-la-Bataille, on the southeast and south (from Castillon-la-Bataille to Libourne) by the Dordogne plain, and to the west by another flat, though slightly less low-lying, area extending as far as Libourne. Remarkably, these boundaries are practically identical to those laid down in 1289, when Edward I of England first drew up the Saint-Emilion area. A glance at any contour map makes the undulating countryside more than clear: the height differences range from almost 100 metres near the church in the centre to only 10 metres above sea level in the little village of Viognet.

Pomerol is a small appellation, created relatively recently, in 1936. It is one of the few quality districts in Bordeaux where an official hierarchy of *crus* has never been established. But this does not alter the fact that alongside the celebrated Château Pétrus there are various other wines here that enjoy worldwide acclaim. Demand for Pomerol is greater than the supply. Prices are therefore on the expensive side.

Increasingly now, too, the district of Fronsac is mentioned in the same breath as Saint-Emilion and Pomerol. It is producing wines of increasing excellence.

Left Château St-Georges in St-Emilion-St-Georges. This historic château was built in 1774 by Victor Louis, who also built the Grand Théâtre in Bordeaux.

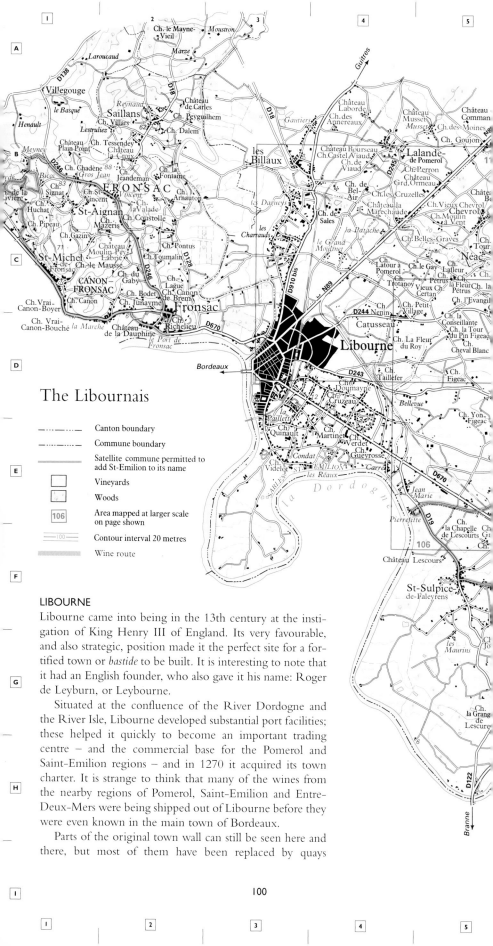

The Libournais

Legend:
- Canton boundary
- Commune boundary
- Satellite commune permitted to add St-Emilion to its name
- Vineyards
- Woods
- 106 — Area mapped at larger scale on page shown
- Contour interval 20 metres
- Wine route

LIBOURNE

Libourne came into being in the 13th century at the insti-
gation of King Henry III of England. Its very favourable,
and also strategic, position made it the perfect site for a fortified town or *bastide* to be built. It is interesting to note that
it had an English founder, who also gave it his name: Roger
de Leyburn, or Leybourne.

Situated at the confluence of the River Dordogne and
the River Isle, Libourne developed substantial port facilities;
these helped it quickly to become an important trading
centre – and the commercial base for the Pomerol and
Saint-Emilion regions – and in 1270 it acquired its town
charter. It is strange to think that many of the wines from
the nearby regions of Pomerol, Saint-Emilion and Entre-
Deux-Mers were being shipped out of Libourne before they
were even known in the main town of Bordeaux.

Parts of the original town wall can still be seen here and
there, but most of them have been replaced by quays

LIBOURNE

🔑 HOTELS

Loubat
32 Rue Chanzy
Tel: 57 51 17 58
A more than adequate hotel with rooms from about FF300. Good simple cooking here with a set menu below FF100.

Auberge les Treilles
11 Rue des Treilles
Tel: 57 25 02 52
Situated in a fairly quiet, small street (parallel to the Rue Chanzy). More than 25 rather modern rooms, modest in size but comfortable (apart from the poor reading light). On warm days, food is served on the terrace outside. Regional dishes. Set menus start at under FF100. Free parking available across the street.

Below and far right There is a thrice-weekly market in the main square of Libourne selling many local delicacies. Cafés are also plentiful in the centre.

bordered by plane trees. It is the confluence of the two rivers that gives Libourne its particular character, however, and parts of the original town, including the Tour de Grand Port, are to be found near this salient feature.

Libourne deserves to be toured on foot. Motorists who drive quickly through are greatly mistaken in doing so. The beautifully restored Carmelite chapel alone, which now serves as an exhibition centre, more than justifies a stop to look round. The Rue des Murs, Rue du Port-Coiffe, and Rue des Chais date back to Libourne's 13th-century origins. So does Rue Carreyron: a medieval street and another of the main places of interest – also well worth a visit. In the Place Abel Surchamp stands the 15th-century town hall, restored in the early 1900s. It houses a number of interesting items, including the Livre Velu, a calf-bound book containing the various enactments of the town and its district, drawn up by the kings of England between the 13th and 15th centuries. In the same square is the Musée des Beaux-Arts with a fine collection of paintings to peruse – including works from the Flemish and Italian schools of the 16th century. The square itself is surrounded

RESTAURANTS

LIBOURNE
Le Chai
20 Place Decazes
Tel: 57 51 13 59
Simple restaurant with regional dishes at favourable prices.
Chanzy
16 Rue Chanzy
Tel: 57 51 05 15
Modest bistro with reasonable food. Set menus start from around FF80.

SABLON-DE-GUITRES
Auberge de l'Isle
Tel: 57 69 22 58
Good cuisine here, with classic dishes of the region including *Terrine de foie au Sauternes* and *Côte de boeuf sur la braise*. There are seven simple rooms below the FF200 mark.

by houses and arcading. A bustling market is held there three days a week.

Some of Libourne's most important wine businesses are situated on the Quai Priourat overlooking the Dordogne. This wine trade quay, which could be compared to the Quai des Chartrons in Bordeaux, has kept much of its original character. The *chais*, covering an area of some hectares, extend far back behind the simple frontages. The words 'Les Amis du Vin' appear on some of them, indicating a mail-order business that also has a shop on the quay.

ST-EMILION

HOTELS

Château Grand Barrail
Tel: 57 55 37 00
Beautifully restored after 30 years of
neglect. Extremely comfortable rooms
(in the castle itself as well as a new
wing) for around FF850. Set dinner
from FF200; lunch is cheaper. Mainly
classic dishes. Wonderful place to stay.

Hostellerie de Plaisance
Tel: 57 24 72 32
Comfortable, and unique in its central
position. All rooms are named after a
château, and some have spectacular

bathrooms. Prices from around FF500.
Cooking sometimes varies. Impressive
wine list with the region's good names.
Table d'hôte starts at around FF130.

Logis des Remparts
Tel: 57 24 70 43
Good hotel in centre; 15 comfortable
rooms. Prices from FF350.

Otelinn
Tel: 57 51 52 05
Modern hotel on the road from
Libourne to Castilllon-la-Bataille: quiet
and comfortable. Rooms from FF300.

Palais Cardinal
Tel: 57 24 72 39
Excellent hotel-restaurant in the
medium range. Rooms from FF300.

*Above, right and far right Scenes
from Libourne, a large town of
25,000 inhabitants, founded in the
13th-century by the Englishman,
Roger de Leyburn, after whom the
town was named.*

Dealing in wine actually started considerably later in
Libourne than in Bordeaux. One of the reasons for this was
the distance from Libourne down to the River Gironde,
which corresponded to one whole tide. A sailing ship therefore needed three tides to get from the river mouth at the
Atlantic up to Libourne – in practice, two days. The spirit
of commercial enterprise seems to have eventually arrived
with settlers from the poorer Corrèze *département* at the
beginning of the 20th century. Families such as Moueix and
Janoueix settling at this time still remain today. According
to official statistics there are now more than 250 wine
businesses in Libourne, but this figure does seem rather on
the high side.

As for viticulture, there are in fact hardly any vines left in
or around Libourne itself. The expansion of the town has
taken its toll and many of the vineyards have disappeared to
make way for new houses and businesses. A few still exist in
the outskirts, however; thus about 160 hectares of the Saint-
Emilion appellation are on Libourne territory, and AC
Pomerol, too, includes vineyards within the municipal
boundaries. In addition, Libourne makes a good base for
exploring the Fronsac wine district, which begins immediately across the bridge near the Tour du Grand Pont. From
there the D670 leads to more wine regions waiting to be
explored: Saint-André-de-Cubzac, Bourg and Blaye (*see*
pages 127–135).

It is amazing that a town like Libourne should be so short of really good restaurants. Saint-Emilion is much better provided for and if you are staying in Libourne, it is worthwhile driving there for a good meal. Another possibility is to be found in the little village of Sablon-de-Guîtres. To get there take the D910 Angoulême road, and then when nearly at Coutras turn left for Guîtres. The distance is only 20 kilometres, and once you get there, you can dine right royally on the banks of the Isle at the Auberge de l'Isle.

RESTAURANTS

Francis Goullée
Tel: 57 24 70 49
Outstanding cuisine in a pleasant restaurant. Classic dishes interpreted in a modern way. Set menus from FF120 and a good, conveniently arranged wine list. Proprietor Goullée often cooks at the châteaux.

Le Clos du Roy
Tel: 57 74 41 55
Restaurant with a rising reputation for its inventive cooking, such as *homard en barquette de tomate*, or *dorade rôtie sur lie de vin*. Cheapest set menu just over FF100.

l'Envers du Décor
Tel: 57 74 46 31
A real, classic *bistrot à vins*, or wine bar. Many wines sold by the glass, from other districts and other parts of the world as well. Classic cuisine attuned to wine. Service on the terrace on warm days. Set menus from about FF100.

SPECIAL INTEREST

From April to the end of September a little train runs through the streets of St-Emilion and the surrounding vineyards. The departure point is the collegiate church on the northwest side of the town, not far from the Place du Marché. The ride lasts for half an hour.

The macaroons from the *pâtissier* Blanchez are regarded as the best. You will find the shop in the Rue Guadet, next to the post office.

In the summer months, information about wine can usually also be obtained at the Pavillon d'Accueil at St-Etienne-de-Lisse, and the Pavillon du Vin at St-Pey-d'Armens.

Saint-Emilion

Right *The beautiful, tiered hillside town of St-Emilion attracts thousands of visitors every year.*

SAINT-EMILION
The town

Medieval Saint-Emilion is one of the most romantic and photogenic wine communities in the world. It lies on the slopes and top of a limestone plateau where building stone for churches, monasteries, fortifications and dwellings was once quarried. The result is a network of passages and chambers in the rock, both under the town and extending right out under the surrounding vineyards. In some cases it is even possible to walk along an underground passage from one château to another. Some of the rock chambers are so huge that banquets can be held in them for hundreds of people – this happens at Château Villemaurine on the edge of the town. Naturally enough many of these caves and passageways have been used for generations now for storing wine. A striking feature of some of them is the vine roots – including some of Saint-Emilion's best – appearing in their ceilings, poking through from the vineyards up above on the limestone.

In times of war the quarries have served as hiding places. In 1793 the tiny town was a place of refuge for a number of Bordeaux deputies pursued by republican extremists. One of these refugees was Marguerite-Elie Guadet, who was tracked down and executed. Her name appears in the Rue Guadet (the main street) and in Château Guadet-Saint-Julien.

Once again, it was the Romans who started winegrowing here. Traces of what were probably Roman vineyards can still be seen at the châteaux of Bellevue and Soutard. Also, the poet and consul Ausonius had one of his three villas in the neighbourhood – possibly where Château Ausone stands today.

Above *Looking down across the rooftops of St-Emilion.*
Below right and far right *St-Emilion has an excellent selection of bars and restaurants.*

ST-EMILION (continued)

RECOMMENDED PRODUCERS

Château Angélus
Grand Cru Classé
Tel: 57 74 42 78
Full, rich St-Emilion with much depth and an agreeable aftertaste with a touch of wood.

Château l'Annonciation
Wine of impressive rounded quality: smooth, generous properties based on a backing of wood.

Château l'Arrosée
Grand Cru Classé
Tel: 57 24 70 47
Distinguished wine with deep colour and a fine, generous taste: vineyards on southwest slope of the plateau.

Château Ausone
Premier Grand Cru Classé (A)
Tel: 75 24 70 26 or 57 24 70 94
Showplace of the Côtes and one of only two Premiers Grands Crus Classés 'A'. The estate, named after Roman consul and poet, Ausonius, is on the edge of St-Emilion's limestone plateau, commanding long vineyard and Dordogne Valley views. Its penetratingly perfumed wines can rival great Médocs in style and finesse.

The name of the town itself comes from Saint-Aemilianus (Emilion), who in the 8th century broke his pilgrim's journey to Santiago de Compostela here, and did not leave. He began to live as a hermit, gathering followers around him. The cave he inhabited is still there and can be visited. Later the Franciscans and Dominicans founded monasteries near the site, and Saint-Emilion was administered jointly by an ecclesiastical chapter and a secular body, the Jurade. In 1289 Edward I of England confirmed Saint-Emilion's status and also defined the area of its jurisdiction. This largely corresponds with the later boundaries of the wine district.

During the Hundred Years War (finally decided in favour of the French, in 1453) Saint-Emilion suffered great damage. A monastery church was almost totally destroyed. All that is left today from this time is a solitary high wall on the northwest side of the town, the Grandes Murailles monument.

The Jurade is still active, although exclusively now in the field of wine. Since being re-established in 1948 it has been engaged in representing and promoting the interests of the local vignerons. Two of the most important events in which the Jurade is involved are the judging of the new wines in June, and the declaration of the grape harvest, the *ban des vendanges*, in September. At this time the members walk through the old streets in their scarlet robes, making a colourful, photo-worthy spectacle.

The whole of Saint-Emilion has been declared a historic monument and use of motor vehicles by non-residents is banned in practically all the streets. Large car parks have therefore been laid out on the edge of the town, outside its former walls. There is so much to see in Saint-Emilion that an hour or two should certainly be set aside for a walk around. It may be a good idea to start by collecting the literature in the Office du Tourisme, which organizes guided tours. Round the corner from this office is the Maison du Vin. All possible information on the wine can be obtained here, as well as details on visiting the châteaux. Anyone who is deeply interested in the Saint-Emilion wines can attend lectures here in the Maison du Vin in the months of July, August and September. It costs around FF100 to do this, and there are sessions twice a day. Those taking part are let into the vinous secrets of the area in a manner that is both instructive and generous. Longer periods of instruction are also possible, an arrangement sometimes combined with meals. The Rue Guadet is where the Syndicat Viticole is established, which looks after the interests of the wine district and its producers.

The tour

A good place to begin your walk around Saint-Emilion is the Place du Clocher, opposite the Office du Tourisme. Adjoining this square is another smaller one, the Place du Marché, with a terrace often packed with colourful sunshades. The Hostellerie de Plaisance, a renowned hotel and restaurant, is in the place du Clocher. It has a wonderful terrace with fabulous views out over the town. The square takes its name from a clocktower 67 metres high. The lowest part of it is 12th-century in origin and is Romanesque; the centre part was built in Gothic style in the 14th century, and the steeple dates from the 15th century. As you wander towards the Place du Marché, you can be easily distracted by the narrow side streets, which reveal a number of wine shops full of tempting bottles. You will also find pastry cooks in Saint-Emilion who make the local macaroons. These little almond cakes

Château Balestard-la-Tonnelle
Grand Cru Classé
Tel: 57 74 62 06
A very old estate – a verse from the 15th-century poet, François Villan, reproduced on the label, refers to 'the divine nectar... of Balestard'. An old stone tower on the estate has been restored and is used for receptions. A big, and at the same time vital, wine, consistent in its soundness.

Château Barberousse
Tel: 57 24 74 24
Estate making firm deep-coloured, generous wine.

Château Beauséjour Duffau-Lagerosse
Premier Grand Cru Classé (B)
Tel: 57 24 71 61
Pretty property on west-facing Côtes. Traditionally made, concentrated wine with a lot of tannin and refinement: demands patience; for laying down.

Château Beau-Séjour Bécot
Tel: 57 74 46 87
In 1984 this estate was deprived of its Premier Grand Cru Classé status for reasons that can only be termed dubious. The wine is still excellent. The château stands high on the plateau of St-Emilion, with fine cellars cut into the limestone.

Château Belair
Premier Grand Cru Classé (B)
Tel: 57 24 70 94
Close to Château Ausone and owned by Madame Heylett Dubois-Challon, co-owner of Ausone. The wine is among the best of the Côtes, with a beautiful aroma of oak and silkiness.

Château Bellevue
Grand Cru Classé
Tel: 57 51 06 07
Fruity wine that lingers nicely, yet firmly on the palate. A classic.

Château Berliquet
Grand Cru Classé
Tel: 57 24 70 71 or 57 24 70 48
A substantial house in a pleasant garden, producing sturdy, harmonious wine with a concentrated aftertaste.

Château Canon
Premier Grand Cru Classé (B)
Tel: 57 24 70 79
Classic St-Emilion of majestic quality
from a partly walled vineyard on the
limestone plateau. It is made in the
traditional way for long cellaring.
Château Canon-la-Gaffelière
Grand Cru Classé
Tel: 57 24 71 33
Deep-coloured wine with lots of fruit
and a harmonious, complex finish.
Château Cap de Mourlin
Grand Cru Classé
Tel: 57 74 62 06
Meaty, richly coloured, quality wine.
Château Cheval Blanc
Premier Grand Cru Classé (A)
Tel: 57 55 55 55
The vineyard of this charming château
is close to the Pomerol boundary and
has a lot of gravel in its soil. The wine
has opulence and refinement, strength
and subtlety. Great vintages are
legendary – unsurpassed even among
the first growths of the Médoc.
Château Clos des Jacobins
Grand Cru Classé
Tel: 56 31 44 44
Relatively supple and firm wine.
Château Clos St-Martin
Grand Cru Classé
Tel: 57 24 71 09
Tiny production here of a great wine
with a taste rich in tannin yet supple.
Château La Clotte
Grand Cru Classé
Tel: 57 24 66 85 or 57 24 72 52
Delicious wine with a pleasant vanilla
character in its bouquet and taste.
Château Corbin-Michotte
Grand Cru Classé
Tel: 56 96 28 57
Harmonious, reasonably firm wine
provided with a finish rich in tannin.
Château Cormeil-Figeac
Tel: 57 24 70 53
Carefully made, rounded, supple wine.
Château Curé Bon la Madeleine
Grand Cru Classé
Tel: 57 74 43 20
One of the mightiest St-Emilions:
broad, intense, sumptuous in taste.
Château Daugay
Noble, generous wine with wood,
vanilla, fruit and a smooth, refined taste.
Château La Dominique
Grand Cru Classé
Tel: 57 51 03 65
Beautiful wine: generous and rounded.
Château Figeac
Premier Grand Cru Classé (B)
Tel: 57 24 72 26
Dignified château with a long history;
the estate once included what is now
Cheval Blanc and other properties.
The vineyard on low gravel hills is 70%

are baked according to a 17th-century recipe from Ursuline
sisters and are the town's only speciality – besides the wine
that is. The Place du Marché does offer some original and
attractive souvenirs, however, in the form of bonsai vines;
there are a number of varieties available.

In this square, too, there is the entrance to the *église mono-
lithe*, the biggest cave church in Europe. It was hewn out by
Benedictine monks in the 11th and 12th centuries. There
used to be frescos on its walls, but most of them disappeared
after the French Revolution, when the church was not only
stripped of its decorations and ornaments, but was also used
to store saltpetre. In 1837 the cave was brought back into use.
Today it is used only for special ceremonies and functions,
such as meetings of the Jurade. It is an impressive, but also a
rather austere, place, and smells of damp and mould. Close
to this monolithic church is the little Chapelle de la Trinité
and, below it, the cave where Emilion lived as a hermit. You
can see the stone bed the saint slept on, his altar, and the

Cabernet (half Sauvignon, the highest proportion for St-Emilion) and the wine has a velvety softness and great allure. It can be drunk early but is capable of long maturing.

Château La Fleur
Grand Cru Classé
Full taste with body to it, an aroma of vanilla and an underlying delicacy.

Château Fonplégade
Grand Cru Classé
Tel: 57 74 12 39 or 57 55 30 20
Distinguished château producing sound juicy, meaty, stylish wine.

Chateau Franc Grace-Dieu
Grand Cru Classé
Tel: 57 24 70 79
Firm, well-structured wine with colour and tannin from the owners of Premier Grand Cru Classé Château Canon.

Château Franc-Mayne
Grand Cru Classé
Tel: 57 24 62 61
Nicely coloured, strong, elegant wine.

Château La Gaffelière
Premier Grand Cru Classé (B)
Tel: 57 24 70 42
A supple, meaty St-Emilion matures in the cellars opposite the large, Gothic château. Reliable wine after 1982.

Château Haut Quercus
Tel: 57 24 70 71
The Union des Producteurs, a coop, scores highly with this wine.

Château Larmande
Grand Cru Classé
Tel: 57 24 71 41
A pithy, slow-developing, quality wine.

Château Magdelaine
Premier Grand Cru Classé (B)
The interest here lies in the wine rather than the property. Magdelaine is hard to equal for flawless quality and a complete and generous taste with a style of its own. The vineyard is 80% Merlot. Belongs to Jean-Pierre Moueix, a Libourne *négociant* that has the greater share in Château Pétrus in Pomerol, amongst others.

Château Mauvezin
Grand Cru Classé
Tel: 57 24 72 36
Wine with a smooth meatiness and an elegant, refined aftertaste.

Château Moulin-du-Cadet
Grand Cru Classé (Libourne)
Wine with strength, charm, refinement.

spring where he quenched his thirst. According to local legend, women could obtain a cure for their infertility by calling on the help of this saint.

The Rue de la Cadène, the little street that leads down-hill from here, is cobbled with stones said to have been brought in as ballast by English ships sailing here from London to load up with wine.

High above the southern part of the little town rises the tower of Château du Roy. Every year the Jurade proclaims the start of the grape harvest from this castle, which has two-metre thick walls. It was built by Henry III of England and is the only surviving donjon, or keep, in the Gironde. In the higher, northern part of Saint-Emilion you can drink a glass of locally made sparkling wine amongst the ruins (and what is left of the cloisters) of the 14th-century Couvent des Cordeliers (Monastery of the Grey Friars). Nearby is the Porte de la Cadène, with its Gothic arches. Walking on northwards, you come to the Porte Bourgeoise, with the

Above and below *St-Emilion is full of historic details at every turn and is perfect for exploring on foot.* Far right *Biscuits d'Amande are a local speciality made from ground almonds, sugar and egg whites.* Right *Château Cheval Blanc is situated close to the boundary with Pomerol.*

Château Pavie
Premier Grand Cru Classé (B)
Tel: 57 55 43 43
On the southwest slope of the plateau; cellars are hewn from limestone, with vine-roots growing through the ceiling. Stylish, supple fragrant wine.
Château Puy-Razac
Grand Cru Classé
Tel: 57 24 73 32
Exemplary wine with stylish meatiness.
Château Rolland-Mailland
Wine with depth of colour, generous taste, and firm structure.
Château Soutard
Grand Cru Classé
Tel: 57 24 72 23
Elegant, likeable wine from larger estate.
Château Tertre Daugay
Grand Cru Classé
Tel: 57 24 72 15
Plenty of colour, strength, complexity.
Château Le Tertre Rôtebœuf
Concentrated, strong-coloured, meaty, unfiltered wine from late-picked grapes.

ruins of the Palais Cardinal close by. This Romanesque building was the residence of Cardinal de Saint-Luce, first dean of Saint-Emilion.

The surrounding villages

Saint-Emilion itself is the most important, but not the only area covered by this appellation. Wines from eight other communes, or parts of them, can be sold under this name. Most tourists only take in Saint-Emilion, but the other villages deserve a visit too – not least because their settings are often attractive and they are frequently more peaceful.

You could begin your tour in Saint-Christophe-des-Bardes (see map on page 101), northeast of Saint-Emilion.

It has a Romanesque church with many (rather weathered) sculptures and reliefs, and has been declared a historic monument. Here also is Château Laroque, one of the oldest in the district – as is clear from the medieval tower. The main building dates from the 18th century.

Nearby at Château Ferrande you can go underground – part of the system of passages to explore is prehistoric – and there is also a spring. Then there is Saint-Hippolyte's 14th-century village church, standing on a hill. You should now take the D245 to Saint-Etienne-de-Lisse, which has a fortified Romanesque church. The village is beautifully situated at the foot of a limestone plateau. Continue the tour by following the D670 in the Libourne direction and then taking

the turning to Saint-Sulpice-de-Faleyrens. The church at Saint-Sulpice is 11th-century. Between this church and Pierrefitte is Château Lescours, where a number of French kings have stayed, among them Henry of Navarre. North of Saint-Sulpice, near the little river harbour of Pierrefitte, is the best-preserved menhir in the *département*. It is a block of stone standing about five metres high and three metres wide, shaped like a hand, and more than 5,000 years old. Back in the immediate area of Saint-Emilion you can visit the hamlet of Saint-Martin-de-Mazerat, where there is a picturesque churchyard, and some renowned châteaux, such as Château Canon, nearby.

The wines

The Saint-Emilion wines – exclusively red – are relatively smooth in taste. Most of them are perfectly ready for drinking when they are young, but have sufficient backbone to mature for years in the bottle. The district has its own separate classification system. This was started in 1955 and has been revised a number of times since then. At the top come the *premiers grands cru classé* château, within which group Château Ausone and Château Cheval Blanc enjoy a special status.

Château Troplong Mondot
Grand Cru Classé
Tel: 57 55 32 05
Powerful wine with great elegance, a long finish and fine touches of wood.

Château Villemaurine
Grand Cru Classé
Tel: 57 74 46 44
Generous, concentrated wine – meaty and rich. The splendid cellars host banquets as well as wine.

Couvent des Jacobins
Grand Cru Classé
Tel: 57 24 70 66
Established in a former 13th-century monastery with splendid rock cellars. Outstanding, complete wine with strength, roundness, breeding, tannin, wood and fruit. Good for laying down.

RECOMMENDED PRODUCERS:
THE SURROUNDING VILLAGES

Château Fombrauge
Grand Cru Classé *Tel: 57 24 77 12* (St-Christophe-des-Bardes) Smooth, generous, reliable wine.

Château Puyblanquet-Carrille
Grand Cru Classé *Tel: 57 24 73 32* (St-Christophe-des-Bardes) Dark wine with smooth fruit aromas, a good, lively taste with backbone and a good finish.

Château Jacques Blanc
Tel: 57 40 18 01 (St-Etienne-de-Lisse) In the vanguard of biodynamic wine growing in the area. Great lingering wine with concentrated fruit.

Château de Candale
Tel: 57 24 72 97 (St-Laurent-des-Combes) Wine with freshness, wood (with a hint of vanilla), and generosity.

Château Bonnet
Tel: 57 47 15 23 (St-Pey-d'Armens) An excellent wine in its category, full of taste and of faultless quality.

Pomerol

—·—·—·—	Canton boundary
—··—··—··	Commune (parish) boundary
CHÂTEAU	Top-quality château
Château	Other good château
☐	First-growth vineyard
☐	Other vineyard
☐	Woods
═══25═══	Contour interval 5 metres

Left   Clos du Clocher. This Pomerol property is situated on the high plateau, on deep gravelly soil. The wine is made using 50 percent new oak.

POMEROL

The Pomerol wine district is relatively small, but it is worked by as many as 175 growers. The average area of the holdings is therefore tiny: Château de Sales, Pomerol's largest estate, has 47.5 hectares. Despite the small scale, the appellation includes a number of world-famous wines. In fact Château Pétrus (the best of all the Pomerol châteaux) ranks alongside Château d'Yquem and Burgundy's La Romanée-Conti as one of the most expensive wines in the world, anywhere.

The eight small hamlets (or clusters of houses) that together make up the Pomerol commune are administered from Pomerol-Centre – recognizeable from afar by its church steeple. This structure, with its 100 pillars, replaced the crumbling 12th-century church built by the Knights of Saint-John (later known as the Knights of Malta), the order which at the time of the Crusades offered help and shelter to travellers and pilgrims. Pomerol was a chosen base as it was on one of the pilgrim routes to Santiago de Compostela in the northwest of Spain. There are to this day signposts with Maltese crosses on them marking the old pilgrim way near the châteaux of Beauregard, Moulinet and La Commanderie, and at many other points. The Knights probably stimulated the growing of wine in the Pomerol region too, if only for its use in the Mass and as medicine. This would be why the local wine fraternity was named La

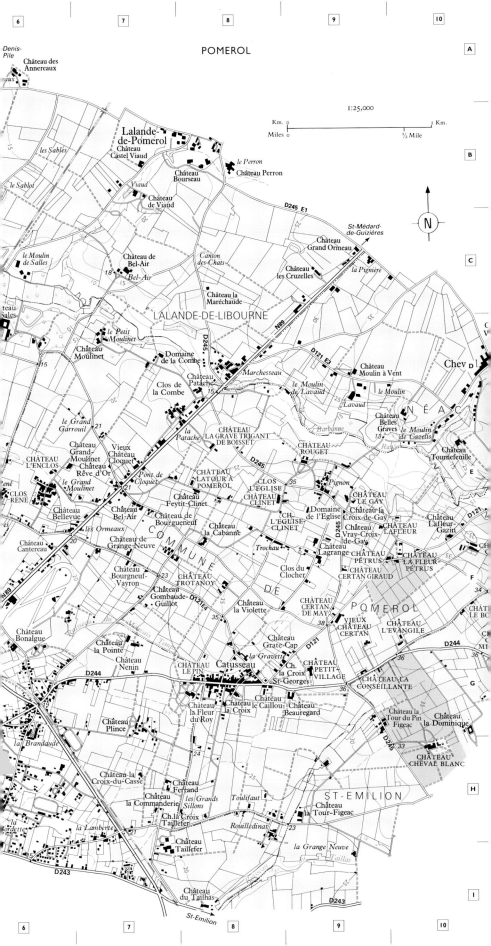

Confrérie des Hospitaliers, and its members have the Maltese cross depicted on their robes.

The taste of many Pomerols makes a more homogeneous first impression than is the case in the wines of the other Bordeaux districts. Most Pomerol wines are more accessible in flavour, more charming, warmer and less reserved in style. And this is all despite the great many variations in the region's soil structure.

In the heart of the district there is a plateau, about 35 metres high, with a superabundance of clay in its soil, mixed in with gravel, forming an important square of vineyards. Here powerful, generous, richly coloured wines are produced: Château Pétrus is the very best of them. Then around this plateau there is a fairly narrow strip of gravel, clay and sand. The wines from vines grown here are robust, intense, but often less rounded and luxurious than those from the plateau. Further west in the district the terrain is flatter and sandier, and the result from these vineyards is comparatively light, supple wines. Another variation in many places is a hard, compact, iron-bearing layer of sand-

POMEROL

RESTAURANT

Chez Servais
Tel: 57 24 31 95 (Artigues-de-Lussac) 'Restaurant de l'Aérodrome', on the N89 between Libourne and Périgueux. A favourite place to eat, especially at lunchtimes. Extensive wine list from Pomerol, St-Emilion and satellites. Set menus start at FF130.

RECOMMENDED PRODUCERS

Château Beauregard
Tel: 57 51 13 36
One of the few grand châteaux in Pomerol, complete with moat, towers and winding stairway. It dates from the 17th century. Elegant, balanced wine.
Château Le Bon Pasteur
Tel: 57 51 10 94
Generous, excellent wine made by well-known oenologist, Michel Rolland.
Château Certan de May
Tel: 57 51 41 53
Exceptionally good Pomerol from a small estate opposite Vieux Château Certan. Wine of firmness and grace.
Château Clinet
Tel: 56 30 10 35 Top class Pomerol.
Château La Conseillante
Tel: 57 51 12 12
Estate on the St-Emilion/Pomerol boundary. Wine with a firm yet exquisite, silky taste of great purity, and a very fine, generous bouquet.
Château La Croix de Gay
Tel: 57 51 19 05
Splendid wine with style and backbone.
Château l'Eglise Clinet
Tel: 57 25 99 00
Richly nuanced wine with deep colour; creamy, rounded and refined style.
Château l'Evangile
Tel: 57 51 15 30
The vineyard (Rothschild-owned since 1990) borders on Château Pétrus and makes a splendid, stylish Pomerol, with a violet-like perfume.
Château La Fleur-Pétrus
Tel: 57 51 78 96
Château with striking egg-yellow shutters. Complex, ageable wine.

stone in the subsoil. This is the *crasse de fer* which is renowned for the special qualities it lends to the wines coming from the vineyards it frequents – it is said to give Pomerols their sometimes truffle-like aroma.

The 17th-century Château Beauregard is a Pomerol wine estate well worth a visit. It was one of the first properties to arise in the region, and has an imposing château surrounded by a moat and (unusually for Pomerol) extensive grounds. In the 1920s an exact copy of it was built on Long Island for the Guggenheim family.

Top left *Château La Pointe.*
Top *Château La Croix de Gay. In recent years investment in installations and expertise has greatly improved the quality of this château's wines.*

Above *Crusty loaves of bread – a French staple.*
Left *Sheep grazing alongside vineyards in the outlying parts of Pomerol. Sights like this are rare because vines are so widespread in the Libournais.*

Château La Grave
Wine with finesse and a touch of richly ripe fruit in the taste.
Château Lafleur-Gazin
Tel: 57 51 78 96
Broad, soundly constituted wine with deep colour, generosity and juice.
Château Latour à Pomerol
Tel: 57 51 78 96
Almost corpulent, generous Pomerol with a lot of soft tannin and ripe fruit.
Château Petit-Village
Tel: 57 51 21 08
Excellent Pomerol which is anything but *petit*; plenty of fruit in its younger years, with firm wood underneath.
Château Pétrus
Pétrus, for all its fame, will disappoint anyone who is looking for a grand château – until you taste the wine. Pétrus is the Pomerol of Pomerols: a dark, exceptionally intense wine that overwhelms the senses with its power. Its unique class puts its price – three times the price of Médoc first-growths – beyond the reach of ordinary mortals. A Moueix team looks after the vineyard (95% Merlot) and makes the wine (its other Pomerol properties include Feytit-Clinet, La Fleur-Pétrus, La Grave Trigant de Boisset, Lagrange, Latour à Pomerol and Trotanoy).
Château La Pointe
Extensive estate where two roads join – hence La Pointe. The château looks out over a magnificent park with stately old trees. Can make colourful, sinewy wines for laying down.
Château de Sales
Tel: 57 51 04 92
Pomerol's biggest estate with an impressive château and extensive park. Always reliable wine with style, structure, elegance and fine perfume.
Château Trotanoy
Tel: 57 51 78 96
Moueix estate on Pomerol's central plateau. The wine is grander than the country house château: concentrated, deep-coloured, with smooth fruit and meaty power. If Pétrus is the emperor of Pomerol, Trotanoy is the king.
Château La Violette
Tel: 57 51 49 78
Delicious wine that does indeed have a fragrance of violets. A feminine, stylish Pomerol that lingers nicely.
Château Vray Croix de Gay
Tel: 57 51 64 58
Less well-known, intense, elegant wine.
Vieux Château Certan
Tel: 57 51 17 33
The oldest known winery in Pomerol – 16th century. A flawless, charming, stylish wine is made, gaining in fragrance and complexity with time. Easily recognized by its pink cap.

ST-EMILION SATELLITES

HOTEL

Château de Roques
Tel: 57 74 62 18
In Puisseguin, offering an attractive
chambre d'hôte amongst the vineyards.

RECOMMENDED PRODUCERS

LUSSAC-ST-EMILION
Château de Barbe Blanche
Tel: 57 74 60 54
Glorious, rounded, truly substantial wine.
Château du Courlat
Tel: 57 51 20 56 (Libourne)
The Jean Baptiste *cuvée* comes from
old vines; it is richly structured with a
refined, yet powerful taste.
Château Mayne-Blanc
Tel: 57 74 60 56
Satisfyingly mouth-filling St-Vincent
cuvée, with good tannins on the finish.

Château Vieux Busquet
Tel: 57 51 03 65 Smooth, rounded wine.

MONTAGNE-ST-EMILION
Château La Fleur Musset
Well-rounded wine with meaty tones.
Château Maison Blanche
Tel: 57 74 62 18 Reliable, structured
wine with smooth finish, rich in tannin.
Château Roudier
Tel: 57 74 62 06 Pleasant, lingering
wine with plenty of juice in the taste.
Vieux Château Négrit
Balanced, meaty wine with long length.
Vieux Château St-André
Tel: 56 39 79 80 (Libourne) Wine
from one of the greatest Libournais
oenologists, Jean Claude Berrouet.
Excellent Montagne-St-Emilion.

PUISSEGUIN-ST-EMILION
Château l'Abbaye
Tel: 57 74 63 12
Powerful aromas; a fruity, tannic wine.
Château Beaulieu
Lively, sound wine that will mature well
in bottle. Reliable, too, in lesser years.

THE SAINT-EMILION SATELLITES

Across the Barbanne stream, which forms the northern boundary of both Saint-Emilion and Pomerol, lie the so-called
satellite districts: the villages of Lussac, Montagne, Puisseguin
and Saint-Georges. Each is allowed to couple its name with
that of Saint-Emilion. Parsac used to be among them but was
subsequently incorporated into Montagne-Saint-Emilion.

Lussac-Saint-Emilion

Lussac lies nine kilometres from Saint-Emilion. In its centre
there is a remarkable representation of an atom made from
wine casks: it is rather less than beautiful. What *is* attractive
is the Maison du Vin, in a 19th-century building with vault-
ing and oak beams. Also, the village church, with a bas-relief
of harvest scenes. Lussac hosts an unusual sporting event: the
international barrel-rolling triathlon where oak wine casks are
propelled along in spectacular fashion. The contest takes place
on the second Saturday in September, and a craft fair and
flea-market is held on the Sunday. There
is also an interesting weekly market on
Thursdays. Other places worth visiting
are Château Lussac and the Picampeau
menhir – known as Pierre des Martyrs –
once used as a sacrificial stone.

Montagne-Saint-Emilion

This is by far the most important of the
satellite districts, at least in volume. In
the middle of the little village there is a
striking church with curious heads over

the main door. Standing on the church steps here you are precisely level with the weather-vane of Saint-Emilion's church (Montagne is on a considerable hill).

In the village, next to the Maison du Vin, there is a wine museum, the Eco-Musée du Vigneron-Paysan. Here you can learn everything about wine and winegrowing... *'tout sur les petites misères et les grands mystères du vin, de la vigne et du vigneron'*.

Puisseguin-Saint-Emilion

The landscape from Lussac to Puisseguin is beautiful, evoking visions of Tuscany with its many hills and groves of cypress trees. The name Puisseguin comes from Puy, meaning 'hill', and Seguin, one of Charlemagne's warriors who settled here in about AD 800. Viticulture dates from some 1,000 years later. The little village is more than usually rustic – the Maison du Vin acts as a tobacconist's, too.

Saint-Georges-Saint-Emilion

The growers of this, the smallest of the satellites, have the choice of using the Montagne-Saint-Emilion appellation or their own. The best wine comes from the finest château for miles around: Château Saint-Georges – a splendid example of Louis XVI architecture. It shows a striking resemblance to the Grand Théâtre in Bordeaux, built in 1770 by the same architect, Victor Louis. The château dominates its surroundings and you can often take your bearings from it as you explore. Saint-Georges itself has a rather exceptional 12th-century church with two storeys, built in Romanesque style on Roman ruins. Notice also the four-storey belltower. The *jardin du curé*, beside this, has some unusual plants.

Far left *Farm-fresh local cheese available from most local markets.*
Above *The church in St-Georges.*
Below *Vines stretch over Puisseguin-St-Emilion.*

Château Branda
Tel: 57 74 62 55 Elegant wine with rich aromas of ripe red berry fruits.
Château Durand-Laplagne
Tel: 57 74 63 07 *Cuvée sélection* is beautifully coloured, with a good, long finish marked by its wood.
Château Lafaurie
Tel: 57 24 33 66 (Artigues-de-Lussac) After undergoing extensive changes and renovations, this estate now makes a strong wine with plenty of tannin.
Château des Laurets
Tel: 57 74 63 40 or 57 74 65 34 Firmly-structured, tannic wine.
Château de Roques
Tel: 57 74 69 56 Long, refined wine.

ST-GEORGES-ST-EMILION
Château Belair St-Georges
Tel: 57 74 65 40 (Montagne) Fine balanced wine that needs a few years.
Château Bellone St-Georges
Tel: 57 74 64 66 (Montagne) Fruity wine with a hint of vanilla smoothness.
Château Calon
Tel: 56 96 28 57 Richly coloured, rounded wine with firm tannin.
Château Cap d'Or
Tel: 57 40 08 88 Well-made juicy wine with a light touch of wood.
Château St-Georges
Tel: 57 74 62 11 (Montagne) The noblest wine of the district; rich, with strength and a generous constitution.
Château Tour du Pas St-Georges
Note the two remarkable wood sculptures outside the cellar.

COTES DE CASTILLON

HOTEL

Hostellerie du Château Lardier
Tel: 57 40 54 11
Pleasant, quiet hotel-restaurant in the hamlet of Ruch. Good rooms from FF220. Good, honest cooking with set menus from FF100–200.

RESTAURANT

La Péniche
Tel: 57 40 30 30
Simple restaurant on the quay beside the Dordogne. Good for a tasty lunch from about FF85.

SPECIAL INTEREST

The annual Castillon-la-Bataille wine fair is usually held in the second half of July. This village also has a Maison du Vin, where details about visits to châteaux can be obtained.

Just outside Castillon, to the east, stands the chapel the French commanders had built in honour of John Talbot, the English leader who fell here in 1453. The battle between the French and the English is re-enacted each year at Belvès-de-Castillon, a little to the north; you can drive there on the D119.

RECOMMENDED PRODUCERS

BELVES-DE-CASTILLON
Château Puycarpin
Tel: 57 97 07 20
Beautifully coloured fruity wine with a concentrated, harmonious aftertaste.

Above *Food being prepared in a simple kitchen in the village of Montagne-St-Emilion.*
Right *A view of a vineyard in the Côtes de Francs, east of St-Emilion. This beautiful area, granted its appellation in 1967, now produces some high quality wines.*
Below *The charming courtyard of the Château de Francs.*

COTES DE CASTILLON

On July 17th 1453 near Castillon a decisive battle was fought between the French and the English. The latter had the worst of it and Aquitaine became French again after three centuries. In 1953 Castillon commemorated the 500th anniversary of this encounter, and 'la Bataille' was added to its name.

Castillon was once an important river port: a fortified town with a large fortress. But only near the Porte de Fer, on the south side by the river, can remains of the town walls be seen. Castillon's church dates from the 18th century, and the *mairie* occupies what was once a hospital.

STE-COLOMBE
Château Poupille
Tel: 57 74 45 30
Wine with a beautiful aroma, tremendously rich in style and tannins. Long, balanced aftertaste with fruit.

ST-LAURENT-DES-COMBES
Domaine des Rochers
Tel: 57 24 70 04
A generous, rich aroma in this wine makes it a sumptuous drink.

ST-MAGNE-DE-CASTILLON
Château Peyrou
Tel: 57 24 72 05
Excellent wine from vines more than 40 years old.

ST-PHILIPPE-D'AGUILHE
Château d'Aguilhe
Tel: 57 40 60 10
Spanish owners.
Château Lamartine
A fine bouquet with a slightly 'animal' hint to it, a pleasing palate with a suggestion of chocolate, and a long, concentrated aftertaste.
Château de St-Philippe
Fine, classic wine with a rounded, balanced taste.

LES SALLES-DE-CASTILLON
Château de Clotte
Tel: 57 40 60 15
This château, with its impressive cellars, produces a soundly structured red wine made in the traditional way.

COTES DE FRANCS

RECOMMENDED PRODUCERS

FRANCS
Château de Francs
Tel: 57 40 65 91
Interesting wine with a rich aroma of red fruits and fine, smooth tannin in the aftertaste.

ST-CIBARD
Les Charmes-Godard
Both red and white wine made. The red had already distinguished itself as a rich wine, and now the white, too, is a discovery: a pleasant nose and a smooth, fruity and exhilarating taste.
Château La Claverie
The property of Nicolas Thienpont, who makes simply amazing wine here.
Château Puyguéraud
Tel: 57 40 61 04
Adjoins La Claverie and is also owned by the Thienpont family. The wine is subtle and elegant, with rich, perfumed aromas.

Today, there is a French airforce base near Saint-Philippe d'Aiguilhe: its radio masts can be seen for miles. Of greater interest, however, is the water tower nearby, open for the public to climb for a marvellous view of the whole region.

There is another vantage point at Sainte-Colombe. Getting there from Saint-Philippe-d'Aiguilhe you can pass through Saint-Genès-de-Castillon, with a stately 15th-century house. Finally, at Saint-Magne-de-Castillon, northwest of Castillon-la-Bataille, there is another church worth seeing.

Castillon wines were elevated from Bordeaux Supérieur to their own appellation in 1989. They rather resemble those of the Saint-Emilion Satellite districts.

COTES DE FRANCS
Côtes de Francs is a small district taking its name from the village of Francs. There is a castle there – the Château de Francs – the oldest parts of which date from the 12th century, the rest from the 14th and 17th centuries. Two Saint-Emilion families produce some notable wines.

Just north of Francs is the hamlet of Tayac, where the remains of a Gallo-Roman settlement have been found and there is a Romanesque church. If you then head south on the D123 it is not far to Saint-Cibard, where there are two leading wine properties (Charmes-Godard and Claverie); the church here is 12th century. West of Saint-Cibard, on a hill near Monbadon, there is a 14th-century feudal castle.

LALANDE-DE-POMEROL

RECOMMENDED PRODUCERS

Château de Bel-Air
Tel: 57 51 40 07
Balanced wine with meaty, fruity tones.

Château Grand Ormeau
Tel: 57 25 30 20 Deeply coloured
wine with an attractive touch of wood.

Château Haut-Goujon
Tel: 57 51 50 05 (Montagne)

Supple, balanced wine, rich in tannin;
good young but also matures well.

Clos des Moines
Supple, generous taste with meat,
and some *terroir*.

Château de Viaud
Tel: 57 51 06 12 (Lalande-de-Pomerol)
One of the oldest estates in Lalande.
Fine, robust wine with a lovely
bouquet and a firm finish.

Château Chevrol Bel-Air (Néac)
Old vines here give a powerful yet
harmonious wine, lightly oaked.

Château les Hauts-Conseillants
(Néac) An estate where
traditional methods are followed,
with flawless results. Wonderfully
aromatic; delicious hints of vanilla and
preserved fruits. A beautiful wine for
laying down.

Château Les Templiers (Néac)
Well-structured wine with light fruit.

Château Vieux Chevrol
(Néac) Full, juicy and mouth-filling
wine with a powerful finish.

*Above The Domaine de l'Eglise
produces highly structured and richly
flavoured Pomerol.*
*Right A change from vines –
woods in the Côtes de Castillon.*
*Far right An old church in the
district of Pomerol.*

LALANDE-DE-POMEROL

This appellation is intended only for wines produced in the communes of Lalande and Néac. These two villages lie north of Pomerol and Saint-Emilion and are separated from them by a little stream, the Barbanne. To the east and south they border on Montagne-Saint-Emilion.

Lalande-de-Pomerol (which is another of the towns on the pilgrimage routes to Santiago de Compostela) has been associated with wine since the 10th or 11th century. The fine little church, with a curious open belfry, dates from a short time after this, in the 12th; a little more recently again, in the churchyard, there stands a cross from the 1400s. The church is the only building hereabouts that has a history from as far back as the time of the Knights of the Holy Cross, and painted in the nave is a list of their rules. Château des Templiers nearby is yet further evidence of their presence.

Lalande wines at one time were classified under Pomerol's appellation, while those of Néac had the designation Néac-Pomerol. Legislation in the 1920s changed this, giving rise to the appellation Lalande-de-Pomerol, and taking away Néac's right to use the Pomerol name. Formally speaking, the separate Néac appellation still exists, although it is no longer applied in practice because in 1954 it was decided that Néac could use the Lalande-de-Pomerol name. The wines of Lalande-de-Pomerol are usually rather less generous, less noble than those of Pomerol, but are clearly related to them – and cost much less.

FRONSAC

RESTAURANT

La Gabarre
Tel: 57 51 99 91
Restaurant by the Dordogne on the
D670, with reasonable fare.
Lunchtime menus start below FF100.

RECOMMENDED PRODUCERS

FRONSAC
Château Barrabaque
Tel: 57 51 31 79
Visits by appointment.
Château Canon
(Libourne)
Distinguished wine with a taste
supported by new wood/some vanilla.
Château Canon de Brem
(Libourne)
One of the most aristocratic wines of
the district.
Château de la Dauphine
Wine rich in flavour with a distinct
suggestion of wood and a long,
balanced aftertaste.
Château Moulin Pey-Labrie
Tel: 57 51 14 37
A very great wine with a rounded,
elegant and harmonious taste.
Château La Grave
Tel: 57 51 31 11
Balanced wine with wood, tannin,
juice and style, from a grower with
totally ecological principles.

LA RIVIERE
Château de la Rivière
A formidable wine, powerful and rich
in tannin on the palate. The quality
reaches at least the level of the better
Médoc *crus bourgeois*.
Château la Rouselle
Tel: 57 24 96 73

SAILLANS
Château Moulin Haut-Laroque
Tel: 57 84 32 07
Very creditable Fronsac with a
spectrum of flavours.
Château Dalem
Tel: 57 84 34 18
A great wine with a deep colour
and rich aroma of red fruit and
liquorice.
Château Fontenil
Tel: 57 51 10 94 (Libourne)
Elegant and refined: fruit on the nose
and a full, complex aftertaste – again
with pronounced fruit character.
Château Villars
Tel: 57 84 32 17
Visits by appointment.

FRONSAC

Near the ancient village of Fronsac, just west of Libourne, a hill rises steeply, fortified at separate points in history by the Gauls and the Romans. Charlemagne built a stronghold on it, which in the following centuries first fulfilled a military function and then became a traffic control point, the owners levying tolls on vessels passing by on the River Dordogne. The castle has been gone now since the 17th century; what remains is a splendid view across Fronsac, numerous châteaux, the river valley, and part of Entre-Deux-Mers.

Anyone driving up or down this hill will pass the Fronsac Maison du Vin, with plenty of information about the local wines and visits to châteaux. Wine is sold here, too.

Fronsac's Romanesque church is a historic monument, and the village has some beautiful buildings to watch out for, dating from the 17th and other centuries past.

Behind Fronsac there lies a romantic winegrowing countryside with winding roads, hills, châteaux, and ever-changing distant views. That viticulture here dates from Roman times is very clear from the remains of one of that period's villas in Saint-Aignan. This hamlet also has a Romanesque church.

ST-MICHEL-DE-FRONSAC
Château Canon
Wine of an unmistakable elegance.
Château Cassagne Haut-Canon
Tel: 57 51 63 98
The ordinary wine has an agreeably
fruity nose, and a rounded taste with
a slight hint of wood; the Cuvée La
Truffiére is more expressive.
Château Mazéris-Bellevue
Tel: 57 24 98 19
People compare this wine to a good
Médoc.
Château Vray Canon Boyer
Sound, full-flavoured wine that is
reckoned to be among the best from
St-Michel-de-Fronsac.

The Château de la Rivière, in
the west of the Fronsac district, is a
large, originally 13th-century castle
flanked by two square towers. It was
built against a high, well-wooded
slope and is very much geared to
receiving visitors. The view from the
château is glorious. The cellars
behind the castle where the wines
are aged make an almost Wagnerian
impact. Visitors pay for admission,
but can retrieve this fee when they
buy a few bottles here.

Adjoining the Fronsac district there is a second, smaller
area called Canon-Fronsac. In the former there are around
120 producers active; in the latter 50 or so. The Fronsac
wines were for a long time unknown, but many growers
invested a great deal in them during the 1980s, and a sometimes spectacular improvement in quality has been the
result. In the matter of wine, Fronsac and Canon-Fronsac
have many a surprise in store.

Main picture *Sun shines on
a quiet street in the village of
Puisseguin.*
Above *Vines at Château de la
Rivière, which dates from the
13th century. This is one of
Fronsac's most important properties,
both visually and in terms of fine
wine production.*

The East Bank of the Gironde

The River Gironde separates two wine districts on its east bank from the Médoc: Côtes de Bourg, and Blaye to the north of it. Both regions take their names from former fortress towns. Blaye was the more important of the two and is today livelier than Bourg, which gives a rather sleepy impression on the whole. It is the red wines of Côtes de Bourg, however, that have in the past had the better reputation. But thanks to present ideas of winegrowing and vinification, both regions are regarded as of equal quality and worth. There is also white Côtes de Bourg, but this amounts to only 5 percent of the region's production. The proportions are quite different in Blaye, for although red wines also predominate here, whites account for 20 percent of what is made. The white wines of Blaye enjoy a particularly good reputation. In general they are not wines of any real refinement, but are easy drinking and are pleasant to drink when they are young. There are nevertheless some surprising exceptions to this rule, and their number is growing steadily but surely.

Bourg lies only 15 kilometres from Blaye, and a visit to the two districts is easiest to begin in the former district, which is nearer to Bordeaux.

Left *The historical town of Bourg with the castle in the foreground. Bourg's strategic importance on the* *River Gironde was first recognized by the Romans; in its time it has been a major fort and a harbour.*

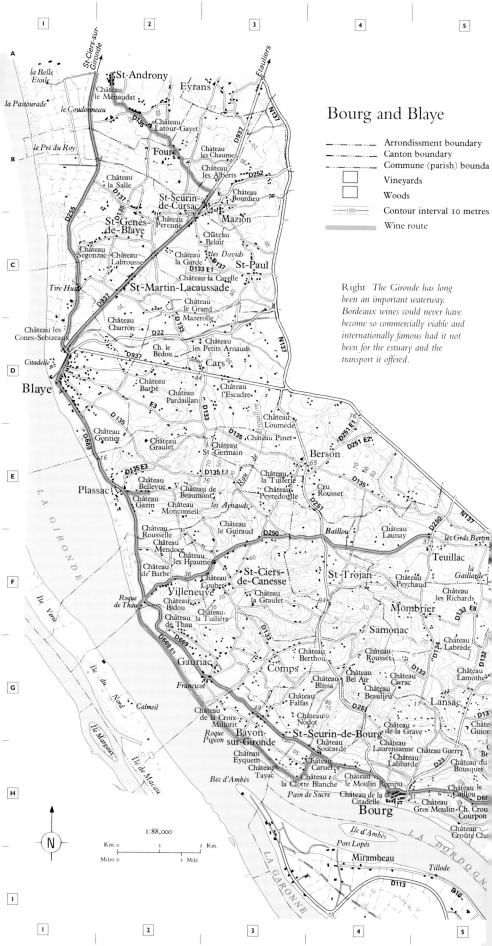

Bourg and Blaye

—–––––––	Arrondissment boundary
—·—·—·—	Canton boundary
—··—··—··	Commune (parish) bounda
▢	Vineyards
▢	Woods
—100—	Contour interval 10 metres
▬▬▬▬	Wine route

Right *The Gironde has long
been an important waterway.
Bordeaux wines could never have
become so commercially viable and
internationally famous had it not
been for the estuary and the
transport it offered.*

la Belle Etoile
la Pastourade
le Coudonneau
le Pré du Roy
St-Ciers-sur-Gironde
St-Androny
Château le Ménaudat
Eyrans
Étauliers
Château Latour-Gayet
Fours
Château les Chaumes
Château les Alberts
Château Bourdieu
Château la Salle
St-Seurin-de-Cursac
Château Perenne
Mazion
St-Genès-de-Blaye
Château Belair
Château Segonzac
Château Labrousse
Château la Garde
les Davids
St-Paul
Château la Carelle
Tire Huit
St-Martin-Lacaussade
Château le Grand Mazerolle
Château les Cones-Sebizeaux
Château Charron
Citadelle
Ch. le Bédou
Château les Petits Arnauds
Cars
Blaye
Château Barbé
Château Pardaillan
Château l'Escadre
Château l'Oumède
Château Gontier
Château Graulet
Château St-Germain
Château Pinet
Berson
Plassac
Château Bellevue
Château de Beaumont
Château la Tuilerie
Château Peyredoulle
Cru Rousset
Château Gazin
Château Monconseil
les Arnauds
Château Rousselle
Château le Guiraud
Baillou
Château Launay
les Grds Bertin
Château Mendoce
Château les Heaumes
Château de Barbe
St-Ciers-de-Canesse
St-Trojan
Teuillac
la Gaillarde
Roque de Thau
Villeneuve
Château Coubet
Château la Graulet
Château Peychaud
Mombrier
Château les Richards
Château Bidou
Château de Thau
Château la Tuilière
Samonac
Château Labrède
Gauriac
Château Berthou
Château Rousset
Château Civrac
Château Lamothe
Comps
Château Bel Air
Château Beaulieu
Lansac
Francicot
Château Blissa
Château Falfas
Château de la Grave
Calmeil
Château de la Croix-Millorit
Château Nodot
Château Guior
Roque Pigeon
Bayon-sur-Gironde
St-Seurin-de-Bourg
Château Soucarde
Château Laurensanne
Château Guerry
Br
Château Eyquem
Château Tayac
Château Caruel
Château Lalibarde
Château du Bousquet
Bec d'Ambès
Château la Clotte Blanche
Château le Moulin Rompu
Château le Caillou
Pain de Sucre
Château de la Citadelle
Château Gros Moulin
Ch. Crou Courpon
Bourg
Château Croûte Cha
Mirambeau
Ile d'Ambès
Port Lopès
Tillode
LA GIRONDE
Ile Verte
Ile du Nord
Ile Margaux
Ile de Macau
LA DORDOGNE
LA GARONNE

N

1:88,000

Km. 0   1   2 Km.
Miles 0   1 Mile

COTES DE BOURG

The hilly landscape of the Côtes de Bourg is referred to as 'the Switzerland of the Gironde'. The district lies on the right bank of the River Dordogne, close to the point where it becomes the Gironde. This charming countryside of rolling hillsides is home to some very agreeable wines, most of which are red.

To reach the Côtes de Bourg district from Bordeaux you can begin on the A10, travelling as far as the Saint-André-de-Cubzac exit and then turning off onto the D669. Another possibility is to go via the D911: this is not so quick perhaps, but has the advantage of taking you through an area that is otherwise apt to be forgotten. The bridge over the Dordogne, built by Gustave Eiffel, is one of the great sights on this route. To the left of the bridge is the Bec d'Ambès industrial complex, on a spit of land formed naturally by alluvial deposits.

After reaching the Côtes de Bourg on the D669 from Saint-André-de-Cubzac (where good Bordeaux and Bordeaux Supérieur wines are produced), there are a number of sights to see. In Prignac-et-Marcamps there is the Pair-non-Pair cave with some 60 prehistoric wall paintings of animals – horses, bison, mammoth and ibex. The cave was discovered in 1881. Within this same commune are the Marcamps quarries. The Prignac district was once an important supplier of limestone, a large proportion of it shipped out from the harbour at Bourg.

If you turn right off the D669 onto the D133, you will soon be in Tauriac, where there is a fine, beautifully restored Romanesque church. There is a large, very active wine cooperative here too.

To visit Bourg, the best way now is to go back to the D669. The official name of this little town used to be Bourg-sur-Gironde, but this is no longer accurate: Bourg is now on the River Dordogne, not on the Gironde, due to the silting up of the river and the formation of the Bec d'Ambès which divides the two waterways.

COTES DE BOURG

 HOTEL

ST-CIERS-DE-CANESSE
La Closérie des Vignes
Very quiet, pleasantly comfortable, charming service. Simple, no-nonsense regional cuisine. Rooms from around FF350, meals from FF125. Swimming pool.

RESTAURANTS

AMBARES
Le Mas du Tillac
Tel: 57 31 75 13
An inn tucked away in an odd corner amongst the vineyards, yet one of the best places to eat in the whole area. Tasty dishes and set menus starting below FF100.

BOURG
Brassserie Le Plaisance
Tel: 57 68 45 34
For a simple lunch on a shadowed triangular terrace near the port (and the cooperative). Inexpensive, good value for money.
Le Troque Sel
Tel: 57 68 30 67
Simple restaurant near the Maison du Vin. Decent, tasty food; set menus from about FF90.

ST-GERVAIS
Au Sarment
Tel: 57 68 30 67
Congenial, rustic restaurant with a leafy terrace. Classic dishes with a modern touch, such as *poêlée d'huîtres au jus de truffes*. Not really cheap, but good. Set menus from around FF120.

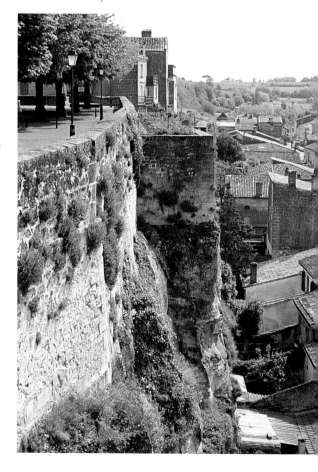

Top *Seafood is plentiful in this part of the Bordeaux region due to its situation on the Gironde.*
Above *One of many charming bars and restaurants in the Côtes de Bourg and Blaye.*

Left *The imposing ancient battlements in Bourg are a dramatic reminder of the region's violent past, when, for centuries, it was fought over by the French and British.*

LE RIGALET
La Filadière
Tel: 57 64 94 05
In this small village on the river there are several restaurants. This is the most attractive, with the best river view and the largest terrace. Set menus start under FF100; Sunday lunch costs around FF130. *Fruits de mer* are a speciality.

RECOMMENDED PRODUCERS

Château Civrac (Bayon)
Wine of a good colour, with a harmonious, promising aftertaste.
Château Falfas
Tel: 57 64 80 41 (Bayon)
Open every day except Sunday.
Château Caruel
Tel: 57 68 43 07 (Bourg)
Juicy, meaty wine with a good balance and discreet fruit.
Château Dumézil (Bourg)
Generally a firm, broad and fragrant wine with some fruit.
Château de la Grave
Tel: 57 68 49 26 (Bourg)
Open every day.
Château Roc de Cambes
(Bourg) Top quality wine.
Château Bujan
Tel: 57 64 86 56 (Gauriac)
There has been great interest in this wine since renovations and reorganization of the château began in 1987. It has a rich, aromatic fragrance and a tremendously luxurious taste.

Château Cantenac Sudre
(Lansac) Compact, dark-coloured
wine with quite a lot of tannin and a
certain style to it. Another prime
example of the quality Côtes de
Bourg can attain.

Château La Croix Davids
Tel: 57 68 40 05 (Bourg)
Open every day.

Château Haut-Gravier
Tel: 57 68 81 01 (Pugnac)
Wine from the Pugnac cooperative,
demonstrating its fine craftsmanship.

Château le Peuy-Saincrit
(St-André-de-Cubzac)
Deep-coloured, mellow wine
provided with plenty of fruit in
bouquet and taste.

Château de Terrefort-Guancard
Tel: 57 43 00 53 (Cubzac-les-Ponts)
Stylish, balanced red wine with a fine
wood element to the taste.

Château Haut-Guiraud
Tel: 57 64 91 39 (St-Ciers-de-Caresse)
Visits by appointment.

Château Macay
Tel: 57 68 41 50 (Samonac)
Wine of a deep but vital red that, in
its smooth bouquet and bright taste,
gives an impression of sweet fruit.
Delightful, especially in its youth. One
of the district's greatest wines.

Château Rousset
Tel: 57 68 46 34 (Samonac)
Smooth elements of new wood give
the Grande Réserve a long, vital and
balanced aftertaste.

Top *The pretty village of
Marmisson, near Blaye, which has
a prehistoric site.*
Above *Although wine tourism in
this part of Bordeaux is
undeveloped, the places of interest
are always well signposted.*
Right *An artist paints the view
across the Gironde estuary.*

Part of Bourg is on a steep chalk escarp-
ment close to the river: a good defensive
position and an unsurprising location for
Roman fortifications – later these were
extended to the whole of Bourg. As a
harbour it was once more important even
than Bordeaux. There is not much left to
see of all that history today. The little
town consists of an upper and a lower
area. In the upper part there is the Maison
du Vin and two adjoining squares with
terraces giving a view across the
Dordogne and the Bec d'Ambès; the lower town is also a
pleasant place to look around. The Château de la Citadelle
used to be lived in by the archbishops of Bordeaux and now
functions as a museum. Beneath it there is a maze of
underground passageways. Also in the lower part of the
town there are some fine houses, as well as a wine shop and
the growers' syndicate.

Not far from Bourg, to the west, is the hamlet of Pain-
du-Sucre where the sparkling wine Crémant de Bordeaux is
produced. In the Blaye direction there is a charming route

to follow that runs close to the riverbank (it meets up with the D669 again before you get to Blaye). You could also stay on the D669, or further explore the wine country of the Côtes de Bourg. The scenery is often lovely, with romantic, vine-clad valleys between the hills. In Teuillac, in the north of the district, there are also 9th-century tombs.

COTES DE BLAYE

Between Bourg and Blaye, about three kilometres south of the latter, is Plassac, where the remains of a Gallo-Roman villa can still be seen. A Gallo-Roman museum has been set up on the site, but it is open only from June to the end of September. Also at Plassac is the Butte de Montuzet, high ground which you can climb for a fine panoramic view of the countryside about. In the village, you should take the road that ascends to Château Bellevue, and do the last bit to the top on foot.

Blaye is also dominated by a hill, albeit a much lower one. The Romans built a fortification here, which they called Blavia. Later a castle rose on the same spot, but this was largely destroyed in the medieval period. The hill is now adorned with a vast citadel, built on the orders of Louis XIV to defend the Gironde against foreign invaders. This stronghold formed a defensive chain with similar forts on the island of Paté in the River Gironde and at Cussac in the Médoc. The architect was Vauban in all cases. The citadel only saw action on one occasion. Later the revenue service had an office here, as any foreign ship wanting to go to

Château Brulésecaille
Tel: 57 68 40 31 (Tauriac)
A taste that is suitably broad and not without tannin, and lingers well. An extremely pleasant, very good Côtes de Bourg that has justly won gold medals.

Château Fongalan
(Tauriac) A usually dark-coloured wine that has a substantial taste and needs to mature three to five years.

Château Querry
(Tauriac) Elegant, balanced wine with backbone and a clean taste. Very pure and among the best in the district.

Château Haut-Macô
Tel: 57 68 40 31 (Tauriac)
Visits by appointment.

Château Perthus
Tel: 57 68 41 12 (Tauriac)
Wine from the local cooperative. Balanced, full of taste with underlying wood.

Château Tour des Graves
Tel: 57 64 32 02 (Teuillac)
One of the rare good white wines from the Côtes de Bourg, with an exciting, exotic taste.

Château Mercier
Tel: 57 64 92 34 (Trojan)
Visits by appointment.

Château de Mendoce
(Villeneuve) A good Côtes de Bourg.

BLAYE

HOTELS

La Citadelle
Tel: 57 42 17 10
A good address, in the fortress itself, with a superb panoramic view across the Gironde. Has some 20 comfortable rooms from around FF300. The cuisine is regionally oriented with a modern touch. Many fish specialities, including *lamproie Bordelaise*. Set menus start at about FF75.

l'Olifant
Tel: 57 42 22 96
Comfortable hotel-restaurant near the D937 to Bordeaux. Simple cooking with a set menu below FF100. The twelve rooms cost less than FF300.

Above Blaye's almost perfectly preserved citadel sits high above the harbour, where the ferry crosses the Gironde to Lamarque.

Right and below right Simple but beautiful buildings are found in Blaye, and there are delightful views of the Gironde across to the Médoc.

Bordeaux had to pay an 'entry fee' at Blaye. And right up to the French Revolution, English crews had to surrender their weapons here.

Although large parts of the citadel badly need restoration, the structure today still remains most impressive. It covers an area of 18 hectares and its walls encompass a camping site, a hotel-restaurant, gardens, a monastery with a chapel, a hospital and all necessary security, including entrances.

According to tradition, it is said the grave of Roland, Charlemagne's nephew, lies somewhere beneath the structure. He is said to have been buried in AD 778 in a church then on the site. There is also a museum of local history and art in the citadel. And as might be expected, there are fine views to be had from the Tour de l'Aiguillette here.

The little town of Blaye itself is made up of straight streets and small squares beside a still-busy harbour, and has an industrious air. The local economy is partly dependent on the presence of a nuclear power station about 20 kilometres to the north at Braud-et-Saint-Louis (this can be visited by appointment: telephone 57 33 32 03).

At Saint-Seurin-de-Cursac, also north of Blaye, there is a museum of prehistory open in the summer at the Château Rolland-Lagarde. In Saint-Ciers-

Château Peyredoulle
Tel: 57 64 39 63 (Berson)
Red wine that is delightful when
young, with small red fruits in the
fragrance and taste; and the
suppleness is there quite early on.
The white has a fresh purity with an
agreeable, somewhat complex taste
of the Sauvignon grape.

Château Crusquet Sabourin
Tel: 57 42 15 27 (Cars)
A generous wine with good
underlying wood and tannin.

Château Gardut Haut-Cluzeau
Tel: 57 42 33 04 (Cars)
Supple red wine that has deservedly
won many medals; and a choice,
exhilarating white.

Château du Grand Barrail
Tel: 57 42 33 04 (Cars)
Classic red wine with a pleasing
element of wood and a delicious
finish. The white is a little
simpler and 100% Sauvignon.

Château les Petits Arnauds
Tel: 57 42 36 57 (Blaye)
Firm-tasting, supple red wine that
lingers in the mouth with a certain
goûte de terroir. Does not require
patient maturing.

Château Marinier
Tel: 57 68 63 13 (Cézac)
Top quality wine.

Château Haut Bertinerie
Tel: 57 68 70 74 (Cubnezais)
Sound red Premières Côtes de Blaye,
with juice, some wood and sufficient
tannin. There is a white wine (also
a sound one) with a reasonably
complex aftertaste.

Château Haut-Grelot
Tel: 57 32 65 98 (St-Ciers-sur-Gironde)
Rich, somewhat fat, supple and
pleasing white wine.

Domaine des Rosiers
Tel: 57 32 75 97 (St-Ciers-sur-Gironde)
Both the red and the white are
agreeable wines; the white has a little
more depth.

Château Charron
(St-Martin-la-Caussade) Exemplary
wine – both the red (Premières
Côtes de Blaye) and the white (Côtes
de Blaye). The red is quite fresh in
taste, supple, with slight fruit; the
white is smoothly fresh and juicy.

Château Les Jonqueyres
Tel: 57 42 34 88 (St-Paul-de-Blaye)
One of the best estates in this region.

sur-Gironde there is a
Romanesque church. Once
you are back in Blaye, a visit
to the Maison du Vin is well
worth while. It is situated in
the centre of town, on the
Cours Vauban. You will find
friendly staff there, and you
will be able to buy regional
wines by the bottle or case
at very reasonable prices.

Various appellations are in
force in Blaye. The red wines, fairly light and often with a
fresh taste to them, are nearly always sold as Premières Côtes
de Blaye; the refreshing whites usually have the Côtes de
Blaye appellation, or sometimes Blayais.

GAZETTEER

GAZETTEER

138

INDEX

Indexer's note: Names of vineyards and wines are often the same and are indexed together eg Ausone, Château 107, 108, 113 where 107, 108 refers to vineyard and 113 to wine. Towns are given in brackets for hotels and restaurants.

INDEX

INDEX

PICTURE CREDITS